Conscious Recovery

Journal

The purpose of *Conscious Recovery* is to offer a spiritual perspective that can assist you in addressing the underlying root causes of your addictive behaviors. It is intended to enhance any program, therapy, or other support system in which you are currently engaged. Its aim is *not* to provide definitive answers, but to introduce questions that can assist you in accessing your own inner wisdom and rediscover your true nature. You are your own best teacher, and you hold the key to ending your own suffering. *Conscious Recovery* can assist you in deepening your understanding of addiction, provide you a roadmap toward liberation, and offer tools to assist you in living your most dynamic and connected life.

This journal is designed to be a companion to the books, *Conscious Recovery*, and the *Conscious Recovery Workbook*, but can certainly stand on its own as a recovery tool. The *Conscious Recovery* journaling process includes a daily inspirational quote, as well as an opportunity to set an intention for your day. At the end of each day, you are given a chance to reflect on your day by exploring the "high point" and "low point" of your day, as well as spending a bit of time reflecting on gratitude.

We are so grateful you have chosen to take this journey with us.
You have the power within you to shift your life.
We hope this journal helps.

TJ Woodward

Table of Contents

January ....pg. 04

February ....pg. 35

March ....pg. 64

April ....pg. 95

May ....pg. 125

June ....pg. 156

July ....pg. 186

August ....pg. 217

September ....pg. 248

October ....pg. 278

November ....pg. 309

December ....pg. 339

January 1

"This moment holds everything you need to awaken to a life filled with passion and purpose."

— TJ Woodward

MORNING

My intention for today is:

_____

_____

_____

NIGHTTIME

The high point of my day was:

_____

_____

_____

The low point of my day was:

_____

_____

_____

Today, I am (was) grateful for:

_____

_____

_____

January 2

"Each day you wake up, say: 'What miracles will you have me perform today?' Then listen."

— Gabrielle Bernstein

MORNING

My intention for today is:

_____

_____

_____

NIGHTTIME

The high point of my day was:

_____

_____

_____

The low point of my day was:

_____

_____

_____

Today, I am (was) grateful for:

_____

_____

_____

January 3

"The key to experiencing peace and wholeness
is living beyond your stories."

– TJ Woodward

MORNING

My intention for today is:

_____

_____

_____

NIGHTTIME

The high point of my day was:

_____

_____

_____

The low point of my day was:

_____

_____

_____

Today, I am (was) grateful for:

_____

_____

_____

January 4

*"Often it is the deepest pain which empowers you
to grow into your highest self."*

— Karen Salmansohn

MORNING

My intention for today is:

_____

_____

_____

NIGHTTIME

The high point of my day was:

_____

_____

_____

The low point of my day was:

_____

_____

_____

Today, I am (was) grateful for:

_____

_____

_____

January 5

"The spiritual journey is about identifying and letting go of old beliefs that no longer serve you."

— TJ Woodward

MORNING

My intention for today is:

_____

_____

_____

NIGHTTIME

The high point of my day was:

_____

_____

_____

The low point of my day was:

_____

_____

_____

Today, I am (was) grateful for:

_____

_____

_____

January 6

"We don't stop playing because we grow old.
We grow old because we stop playing."
— George Bernard Shaw

MORNING

My intention for today is:

_____

_____

_____

NIGHTTIME

The high point of my day was:

_____

_____

_____

The low point of my day was:

_____

_____

_____

Today, I am (was) grateful for:

_____

_____

_____

January 7

*"We strive and push because we've been programmed
to see life through the lens of scarcity."*

— TJ Woodward

MORNING

My intention for today is:

_____

_____

_____

NIGHTTIME

The high point of my day was:

_____

_____

_____

The low point of my day was:

_____

_____

_____

Today, I am (was) grateful for:

_____

_____

_____

January 8

"A miracle is a shift in perspective
from fear to love."

– Marianne Williamson

MORNING

My intention for today is:

_____

_____

_____

NIGHTTIME

The high point of my day was:

_____

_____

_____

The low point of my day was:

_____

_____

_____

Today, I am (was) grateful for:

_____

_____

_____

January 9

*"In the silence, we can recognize that we have thoughts,
but we are not our thoughts."*

– TJ Woodward

MORNING

My intention for today is:

_____

_____

_____

NIGHTTIME

The high point of my day was:

_____

_____

_____

The low point of my day was:

_____

_____

_____

Today, I am (was) grateful for:

_____

_____

_____

January 10

"You are not a drop in the ocean.
You are the entire ocean in a drop."

– Rumi

MORNING

My intention for today is:

_____

_____

_____

NIGHTTIME

The high point of my day was:

_____

_____

_____

The low point of my day was:

_____

_____

_____

Today, I am (was) grateful for:

_____

_____

_____

January 11

"Nonresistance is a practice that allows us to truly experience present moment awareness."

— TJ Woodward

MORNING

My intention for today is:

_____

_____

_____

NIGHTTIME

The high point of my day was:

_____

_____

_____

The low point of my day was:

_____

_____

_____

Today, I am (was) grateful for:

_____

_____

_____

January 12

"Eventually you will come to understand that love heals everything, and love is all there is."

— Gary Zukav

MORNING

My intention for today is:

_____

_____

_____

NIGHTTIME

The high point of my day was:

_____

_____

_____

The low point of my day was:

_____

_____

_____

Today, I am (was) grateful for:

_____

_____

_____

January 13

"We learn a great deal when we simply sit with our thoughts - not in judgment, but in observation."

— TJ Woodward

MORNING

My intention for today is:

_____

_____

_____

NIGHTTIME

The high point of my day was:

_____

_____

_____

The low point of my day was:

_____

_____

_____

Today, I am (was) grateful for:

_____

_____

_____

January 14

"Expect great things, then let go
of how they show up."

— Panache Desai

MORNING

My intention for today is:

_____

_____

_____

NIGHTTIME

The high point of my day was:

_____

_____

_____

The low point of my day was:

_____

_____

_____

Today, I am (was) grateful for:

_____

_____

_____

January 15

*"Your thoughts, ideas, and viewpoints are not
as solid as you might believe."*

— TJ Woodward

MORNING

My intention for today is:

_____

_____

_____

NIGHTTIME

The high point of my day was:

_____

_____

_____

The low point of my day was:

_____

_____

_____

Today, I am (was) grateful for:

_____

_____

_____

January 16

"Don't look for your dreams to come true; look
to become true to your dreams."

— Michael Beckwith

MORNING

My intention for today is:

_____

_____

_____

NIGHTTIME

The high point of my day was:

_____

_____

_____

The low point of my day was:

_____

_____

_____

Today, I am (was) grateful for:

_____

_____

_____

January 17

"We are not built to live in isolation and live cut off from love and connection."

— TJ Woodward

MORNING

My intention for today is:

_____
_____
_____

NIGHTTIME

The high point of my day was:

_____
_____
_____

The low point of my day was:

_____
_____
_____

Today, I am (was) grateful for:

_____
_____
_____

January 18

*"Nothing every goes away until it has taught
us what we need to know."*

— Pema Chodron

MORNING

My intention for today is:

_____

_____

_____

NIGHTTIME

The high point of my day was:

_____

_____

_____

The low point of my day was:

_____

_____

_____

Today, I am (was) grateful for:

_____

_____

_____

January 19

"Real strength and real power, is about steering the ship of life, rather than forcing it through the water."

— TJ Woodward

MORNING

My intention for today is:

_____

_____

_____

NIGHTTIME

The high point of my day was:

_____

_____

_____

The low point of my day was:

_____

_____

_____

Today, I am (was) grateful for:

_____

_____

_____

January 20

"We live in a world of outrageous pain. The only response to outrageous pain is outrageous love."

– Marc Gafini

MORNING

My intention for today is:

_____

_____

_____

NIGHTTIME

The high point of my day was:

_____

_____

_____

The low point of my day was:

_____

_____

_____

Today, I am (was) grateful for:

_____

_____

_____

January 21

"Living with a closed heart is not an effective long-term solution."

— TJ Woodward

MORNING

My intention for today is:

_____

_____

_____

NIGHTTIME

The high point of my day was:

_____

_____

_____

The low point of my day was:

_____

_____

_____

Today, I am (was) grateful for:

_____

_____

_____

January 22

"The first half of life is devoted to forming a healthy ego.
The second half is going inward and letting it go."

– Carl Jung

MORNING

My intention for today is:

_____

_____

_____

NIGHTTIME

The high point of my day was:

_____

_____

_____

The low point of my day was:

_____

_____

_____

Today, I am (was) grateful for:

_____

_____

_____

January 23

"We don't grow spiritually so much as we grow in awareness of our spiritual essence."

— TJ Woodward

MORNING

My intention for today is:

_____

_____

_____

NIGHTTIME

The high point of my day was:

_____

_____

_____

The low point of my day was:

_____

_____

_____

Today, I am (was) grateful for:

_____

_____

_____

January 24

"People say walking on water is a miracle. But to me walking peacefully on the earth is the real miracle."

– Thich Nhat Hanh

MORNING

My intention for today is:

_____

_____

_____

NIGHTTIME

The high point of my day was:

_____

_____

_____

The low point of my day was:

_____

_____

_____

Today, I am (was) grateful for:

_____

_____

_____

January 25

"Repeatedly saying 'I am a victim' or 'I am powerless' only concretizes victim mentality into your consciousness."

– TJ Woodward

MORNING

My intention for today is:

_____

_____

_____

NIGHTTIME

The high point of my day was:

_____

_____

_____

The low point of my day was:

_____

_____

_____

Today, I am (was) grateful for:

_____

_____

_____

January 26

*"We can complain that rose bushes have thorns,
or rejoice because thorn bushes have roses."*

— Abraham Lincoln

MORNING

My intention for today is:

_____

_____

_____

NIGHTTIME

The high point of my day was:

_____

_____

_____

The low point of my day was:

_____

_____

_____

Today, I am (was) grateful for:

_____

_____

_____

January 27

"We all have heartbreaking stories. The question is: are we going to let them break our heart open?"

— TJ Woodward

MORNING

My intention for today is:

_____

_____

_____

NIGHTTIME

The high point of my day was:

_____

_____

_____

The low point of my day was:

_____

_____

_____

Today, I am (was) grateful for:

_____

_____

_____

January 28

"Never worry about numbers. Help one person at a time and always start with the person nearest you."

– Mother Teresa

MORNING

My intention for today is:

_____

_____

_____

NIGHTTIME

The high point of my day was:

_____

_____

_____

The low point of my day was:

_____

_____

_____

Today, I am (was) grateful for:

_____

_____

_____

January 29

"With conscious awareness, we're able to look at our reactions compassionately, and then move beyond them."

— TJ Woodward

MORNING

My intention for today is:

_____

_____

_____

NIGHTTIME

The high point of my day was:

_____

_____

_____

The low point of my day was:

_____

_____

_____

Today, I am (was) grateful for:

_____

_____

_____

January 30

"Your task is not to seek for love, but merely to seek and find all the barriers within yourself you have built against it."

— Rumi

MORNING

My intention for today is:

_____

_____

_____

NIGHTTIME

The high point of my day was:

_____

_____

_____

The low point of my day was:

_____

_____

_____

Today, I am (was) grateful for:

_____

_____

_____

January 31

"The only way to permanently break free from addiction is to have a dramatic shift in the way you relate to yourself."

— TJ Woodward

MORNING

My intention for today is:

_____

_____

_____

NIGHTTIME

The high point of my day was:

_____

_____

_____

The low point of my day was:

_____

_____

_____

Today, I am (was) grateful for:

_____

_____

_____

February 1

*"Forgiveness allows us to eradicate our stories
of blaming and victimization."*

– TJ Woodward

MORNING

My intention for today is:

_____

_____

_____

NIGHTTIME

The high point of my day was:

_____

_____

_____

The low point of my day was:

_____

_____

_____

Today, I am (was) grateful for:

_____

_____

_____

February 2

"Never doubt that a small group of thoughtful, committed people can change the world. It is the only thing that ever has."
– Margaret Mead

MORNING

My intention for today is:

_____

_____

_____

NIGHTTIME

The high point of my day was:

_____

_____

_____

The low point of my day was:

_____

_____

_____

Today, I am (was) grateful for:

_____

_____

_____

February 3

*"Recovery calls us to be authentic and to bring
our whole self into the room."*

— TJ Woodward

MORNING

My intention for today is:

_____

_____

_____

NIGHTTIME

The high point of my day was:

_____

_____

_____

The low point of my day was:

_____

_____

_____

Today, I am (was) grateful for:

_____

_____

_____

February 4

"When things aren't adding up in your life,
start subtracting."

– Unknown

MORNING

My intention for today is:

_____

_____

_____

NIGHTTIME

The high point of my day was:

_____

_____

_____

The low point of my day was:

_____

_____

_____

Today, I am (was) grateful for:

_____

_____

_____

February 5

"We break the cycle of addiction by bringing our unconscious patterns into conscious awareness."

– TJ Woodward

MORNING

My intention for today is:

_____

_____

_____

NIGHTTIME

The high point of my day was:

_____

_____

_____

The low point of my day was:

_____

_____

_____

Today, I am (was) grateful for:

_____

_____

_____

February 6

"When you become comfortable with uncertainty,
infinite possibilities open up in your life."

– Eckhart Tolle

MORNING

My intention for today is:

_____

_____

_____

NIGHTTIME

The high point of my day was:

_____

_____

_____

The low point of my day was:

_____

_____

_____

Today, I am (was) grateful for:

_____

_____

_____

February 7

"Addictive behavior is simply a strategy for avoiding what's here now because it seems too painful or shameful."

— TJ Woodward

MORNING

My intention for today is:

_____

_____

_____

NIGHTTIME

The high point of my day was:

_____

_____

_____

The low point of my day was:

_____

_____

_____

Today, I am (was) grateful for:

_____

_____

_____

February 8

"If you don't find God in the next person you meet,
don't waste your time looking any further."

– Gandhi

MORNING

My intention for today is:

_____

_____

_____

NIGHTTIME

The high point of my day was:

_____

_____

_____

The low point of my day was:

_____

_____

_____

Today, I am (was) grateful for:

_____

_____

_____

February 9

"The only thing that blocks us from enlightenment is the belief that we are blocked from enlightenment."

— TJ Woodward

MORNING

My intention for today is:

_____

_____

_____

NIGHTTIME

The high point of my day was:

_____

_____

_____

The low point of my day was:

_____

_____

_____

Today, I am (was) grateful for:

_____

_____

_____

February 10

"If you know how to handle this moment,
you know who to handle eternity."

– Sadhguru

MORNING

My intention for today is:

_____

_____

_____

NIGHTTIME

The high point of my day was:

_____

_____

_____

The low point of my day was:

_____

_____

_____

Today, I am (was) grateful for:

_____

_____

_____

February 11

"Feelings are present for a reason. They are the internal navigation system letting us know something needs attention."
— TJ Woodward

MORNING

My intention for today is:

_____

_____

_____

NIGHTTIME

The high point of my day was:

_____

_____

_____

The low point of my day was:

_____

_____

_____

Today, I am (was) grateful for:

_____

_____

_____

February 12

"Loving people live in a loving world. Hostile people live in a hostile world. Same world."

— Wayne Dyer

MORNING

My intention for today is:

_____

_____

_____

NIGHTTIME

The high point of my day was:

_____

_____

_____

The low point of my day was:

_____

_____

_____

Today, I am (was) grateful for:

_____

_____

_____

February 13

*"The more we practice gratitude, the more life
seems to give us to be grateful for."*

– TJ Woodward

MORNING

My intention for today is:

_____

_____

_____

NIGHTTIME

The high point of my day was:

_____

_____

_____

The low point of my day was:

_____

_____

_____

Today, I am (was) grateful for:

_____

_____

_____

February 14

*"The love you are looking for resides
in your own heart."*

– Unknown

MORNING

My intention for today is:

_____

_____

_____

NIGHTTIME

The high point of my day was:

_____

_____

_____

The low point of my day was:

_____

_____

_____

Today, I am (was) grateful for:

_____

_____

_____

February 15

"We have the power to shift our perception and therefore shift the way we experience life."

— TJ Woodward

MORNING

My intention for today is:

_____

_____

_____

NIGHTTIME

The high point of my day was:

_____

_____

_____

The low point of my day was:

_____

_____

_____

Today, I am (was) grateful for:

_____

_____

_____

February 16

"Every moment, every glance, every word,
can be infused with love."

– Thich Nhat Hanh

MORNING

My intention for today is:

_____

_____

_____

NIGHTTIME

The high point of my day was:

_____

_____

_____

The low point of my day was:

_____

_____

_____

Today, I am (was) grateful for:

_____

_____

_____

February 17

"As you grow in spiritual awareness, your perspective will shift to the limitless possibilities of life."

– TJ Woodward

MORNING

My intention for today is:

_____

_____

_____

NIGHTTIME

The high point of my day was:

_____

_____

_____

The low point of my day was:

_____

_____

_____

Today, I am (was) grateful for:

_____

_____

_____

February 18

"What a liberation to realize that 'the voice in my head' is not who I am. Who am I then? The one who sees that."

– Eckhart Tolle

MORNING

My intention for today is:

_____

_____

_____

NIGHTTIME

The high point of my day was:

_____

_____

_____

The low point of my day was:

_____

_____

_____

Today, I am (was) grateful for:

_____

_____

_____

February 19

"Meditation is a practice. What are we practicing?
A new way of being in the world."

— TJ Woodward

MORNING

My intention for today is:

_____

_____

_____

NIGHTTIME

The high point of my day was:

_____

_____

_____

The low point of my day was:

_____

_____

_____

Today, I am (was) grateful for:

_____

_____

_____

February 20

"Lighthouses don't go running all over an island looking for boats to save; they just stand there shining."

— Anne Lamott

MORNING

My intention for today is:

_____

_____

_____

NIGHTTIME

The high point of my day was:

_____

_____

_____

The low point of my day was:

_____

_____

_____

Today, I am (was) grateful for:

_____

_____

_____

February 21

"Judgments prevent us from experiencing
love and connection."

– TJ Woodward

MORNING

My intention for today is:

_____

_____

_____

NIGHTTIME

The high point of my day was:

_____

_____

_____

The low point of my day was:

_____

_____

_____

Today, I am (was) grateful for:

_____

_____

_____

February 22

*"No problem can be solved from the same level
of consciousness that created it."*

– Albert Einstein

MORNING

My intention for today is:

_____

_____

_____

NIGHTTIME

The high point of my day was:

_____

_____

_____

The low point of my day was:

_____

_____

_____

Today, I am (was) grateful for:

_____

_____

_____

February 23

"Every experience in life can be used as
fuel for our transformation."

– TJ Woodward

MORNING

My intention for today is:

_____

_____

_____

NIGHTTIME

The high point of my day was:

_____

_____

_____

The low point of my day was:

_____

_____

_____

Today, I am (was) grateful for:

_____

_____

_____

February 24

"And those who were seen dancing were thought to be insane by those who could not hear the music."

– Friedrich Nietzsche

MORNING

My intention for today is:

_____

_____

_____

NIGHTTIME

The high point of my day was:

_____

_____

_____

The low point of my day was:

_____

_____

_____

Today, I am (was) grateful for:

_____

_____

_____

February 25

"Recovery means a restoration to health. It is a restoration to your essential self, free from all your limiting beliefs."

— TJ Woodward

MORNING

My intention for today is:

_____

_____

_____

NIGHTTIME

The high point of my day was:

_____

_____

_____

The low point of my day was:

_____

_____

_____

Today, I am (was) grateful for:

_____

_____

_____

February 26

*"Do one thing every day
that scares you."*

– Eleanor Roosevelt

MORNING

My intention for today is:

_____

_____

_____

NIGHTTIME

The high point of my day was:

_____

_____

_____

The low point of my day was:

_____

_____

_____

Today, I am (was) grateful for:

_____

_____

_____

February 27

"Gratitude is not only a feeling –
it's also a way of seeing and being."

– TJ Woodward

MORNING

My intention for today is:

_____

_____

_____

NIGHTTIME

The high point of my day was:

_____

_____

_____

The low point of my day was:

_____

_____

_____

Today, I am (was) grateful for:

_____

_____

_____

February 28

"Close some doors, not because of pride, incapacity, or arrogance, but simply because they no longer lead somewhere."
– Paulo Coelho

MORNING

My intention for today is:

_____

_____

_____

NIGHTTIME

The high point of my day was:

_____

_____

_____

The low point of my day was:

_____

_____

_____

Today, I am (was) grateful for:

_____

_____

_____

February 29

*"If we're stuck seeing the world through the lens of 'us' and
'them' then compassion and forgiveness may seem impossible."*
— TJ Woodward

MORNING

My intention for today is:

_____

_____

_____

NIGHTTIME

The high point of my day was:

_____

_____

_____

The low point of my day was:

_____

_____

_____

Today, I am (was) grateful for:

_____

_____

_____

March 1

"Imagine a world where all human beings knew themselves to be love – what would happen to the world's 'problems?'"

— TJ Woodward

MORNING

My intention for today is:

_____

_____

_____

NIGHTTIME

The high point of my day was:

_____

_____

_____

The low point of my day was:

_____

_____

_____

Today, I am (was) grateful for:

_____

_____

_____

March 2

*"When you realize there is nothing lacking,
the whole world belongs to you."*

– Lao-Tzu

MORNING

My intention for today is:

_____

_____

_____

NIGHTTIME

The high point of my day was:

_____

_____

_____

The low point of my day was:

_____

_____

_____

Today, I am (was) grateful for:

_____

_____

_____

March 3

"Life is a great experiment. Why not try practicing gratitude and see what happens?"

– TJ Woodward

MORNING

My intention for today is:

_____

_____

_____

NIGHTTIME

The high point of my day was:

_____

_____

_____

The low point of my day was:

_____

_____

_____

Today, I am (was) grateful for:

_____

_____

_____

March 4

*"The highest form of human intelligence is
to observe yourself without judgment."*

– Krishnamurti

MORNING

My intention for today is:

_____

_____

_____

NIGHTTIME

The high point of my day was:

_____

_____

_____

The low point of my day was:

_____

_____

_____

Today, I am (was) grateful for:

_____

_____

_____

March 5

"When we are grounded in our absolute essence, we can respond rather than react to the fluctuations of the world."
— TJ Woodward

MORNING

My intention for today is:

_____

_____

_____

NIGHTTIME

The high point of my day was:

_____

_____

_____

The low point of my day was:

_____

_____

_____

Today, I am (was) grateful for:

_____

_____

_____

March 6

*"Follow your bliss and the universe will open
doors where there are only walls."*

— Joseph Campbell

MORNING

My intention for today is:

_____

_____

_____

NIGHTTIME

The high point of my day was:

_____

_____

_____

The low point of my day was:

_____

_____

_____

Today, I am (was) grateful for:

_____

_____

_____

March 7

"Your freedom is not limited by how things
appear in the external world."

– TJ Woodward

MORNING

My intention for today is:

_____
_____
_____

NIGHTTIME

The high point of my day was:

_____
_____
_____

The low point of my day was:

_____
_____
_____

Today, I am (was) grateful for:

_____
_____
_____

March 8

*"When they attack you and you notice that you love them
with all your heart, your work is done."*

– Byron Katie

MORNING

My intention for today is:

_____

_____

_____

NIGHTTIME

The high point of my day was:

_____

_____

_____

The low point of my day was:

_____

_____

_____

Today, I am (was) grateful for:

_____

_____

_____

March 9

"Nonresistance allows us to take a broader view and ask ourselves if it's possible to see differently."

— TJ Woodward

MORNING

My intention for today is:

_____

_____

_____

NIGHTTIME

The high point of my day was:

_____

_____

_____

The low point of my day was:

_____

_____

_____

Today, I am (was) grateful for:

_____

_____

_____

March 10

"You should sit in meditation for twenty minutes every day –
unless you're too busy; then you should sit for an hour."

– Zen Adage

MORNING

My intention for today is:

_____

_____

_____

NIGHTTIME

The high point of my day was:

_____

_____

_____

The low point of my day was:

_____

_____

_____

Today, I am (was) grateful for:

_____

_____

_____

March 11

*"Spending time in the silence allows you to
be more loving in the world."*

– TJ Woodward

MORNING

My intention for today is:

_____

_____

_____

NIGHTTIME

The high point of my day was:

_____

_____

_____

The low point of my day was:

_____

_____

_____

Today, I am (was) grateful for:

_____

_____

_____

March 12

"People will forget what you said. People will forget what you did. But people will never forget how you made them feel."

– Maya Angelou

MORNING

My intention for today is:

_____

_____

_____

NIGHTTIME

The high point of my day was:

_____

_____

_____

The low point of my day was:

_____

_____

_____

Today, I am (was) grateful for:

_____

_____

_____

March 13

"When you grow in conscious awareness, you naturally access and activate a deeper blueprint for your life."

– TJ Woodward

MORNING

My intention for today is:

_____

_____

_____

NIGHTTIME

The high point of my day was:

_____

_____

_____

The low point of my day was:

_____

_____

_____

Today, I am (was) grateful for:

_____

_____

_____

March 14

"You can only lose something that you have, but you cannot lose something that you are."

– Eckhart Tolle

MORNING

My intention for today is:

_____

_____

_____

NIGHTTIME

The high point of my day was:

_____

_____

_____

The low point of my day was:

_____

_____

_____

Today, I am (was) grateful for:

_____

_____

_____

March 15

"True freedom comes from not being deeply entrenched
or invested in our opinions and perspectives."

— TJ Woodward

MORNING

My intention for today is:

_____

_____

_____

NIGHTTIME

The high point of my day was:

_____

_____

_____

The low point of my day was:

_____

_____

_____

Today, I am (was) grateful for:

_____

_____

_____

March 16

"If we do not feel grateful for what we already have, what makes us think we'd be happy with more?"

– Unknown

MORNING

My intention for today is:

_____

_____

_____

NIGHTTIME

The high point of my day was:

_____

_____

_____

The low point of my day was:

_____

_____

_____

Today, I am (was) grateful for:

_____

_____

_____

March 17

"What if everything were perfect just as it is, even with its imperfections? How would that awareness change your life?"
— TJ Woodward

MORNING

My intention for today is:

_____

_____

_____

NIGHTTIME

The high point of my day was:

_____

_____

_____

The low point of my day was:

_____

_____

_____

Today, I am (was) grateful for:

_____

_____

_____

March 18

*"If the only prayer you said in your whole life was
'thank you,' it would suffice."*

– Meister Eckhart

MORNING

My intention for today is:

_____

_____

_____

NIGHTTIME

The high point of my day was:

_____

_____

_____

The low point of my day was:

_____

_____

_____

Today, I am (was) grateful for:

_____

_____

_____

March 19

*"The more connected we are with ourselves,
the more connected we can be with others."*

— TJ Woodward

MORNING

My intention for today is:

_____

_____

_____

NIGHTTIME

The high point of my day was:

_____

_____

_____

The low point of my day was:

_____

_____

_____

Today, I am (was) grateful for:

_____

_____

_____

March 20

"Life is simple. It's what we believe about life that complicates it."

— Byron Katie

MORNING

My intention for today is:

_____

_____

_____

NIGHTTIME

The high point of my day was:

_____

_____

_____

The low point of my day was:

_____

_____

_____

Today, I am (was) grateful for:

_____

_____

_____

March 21

"As our inner vibration of gratitude grows, it naturally manifests in the outer world."

— TJ Woodward

MORNING

My intention for today is:

_____

_____

_____

NIGHTTIME

The high point of my day was:

_____

_____

_____

The low point of my day was:

_____

_____

_____

Today, I am (was) grateful for:

_____

_____

_____

March 22

*"The greatest paradox is that when I accept myself
just as I am, then I can change."*

– Carl Rogers

MORNING

My intention for today is:

_____

_____

_____

NIGHTTIME

The high point of my day was:

_____

_____

_____

The low point of my day was:

_____

_____

_____

Today, I am (was) grateful for:

_____

_____

_____

March 23

*"Nothing outside of you needs to change for you
to be living the best version of your life."*

— TJ Woodward

MORNING

My intention for today is:

_____

_____

_____

NIGHTTIME

The high point of my day was:

_____

_____

_____

The low point of my day was:

_____

_____

_____

Today, I am (was) grateful for:

_____

_____

_____

March 24

*"A boat is safe in the harbor. But that is
not the purpose of a boat."*

– Paulo Coelho

MORNING

My intention for today is:

_____

_____

_____

NIGHTTIME

The high point of my day was:

_____

_____

_____

The low point of my day was:

_____

_____

_____

Today, I am (was) grateful for:

_____

_____

_____

March 25

"If we feel we are not worthy of love, we will sabotage it when it presents itself."

– TJ Woodward

MORNING

My intention for today is:

_____

_____

_____

NIGHTTIME

The high point of my day was:

_____

_____

_____

The low point of my day was:

_____

_____

_____

Today, I am (was) grateful for:

_____

_____

_____

March 26

"This moment is the perfect teacher. And, lucky for us,
it's wherever we are."

— Pema Chodron

MORNING

My intention for today is:

_____

_____

_____

NIGHTTIME

The high point of my day was:

_____

_____

_____

The low point of my day was:

_____

_____

_____

Today, I am (was) grateful for:

_____

_____

_____

March 27

"The more we practice spiritual principles,
the clearer the inner voice becomes."

— TJ Woodward

MORNING

My intention for today is:

_____

_____

_____

NIGHTTIME

The high point of my day was:

_____

_____

_____

The low point of my day was:

_____

_____

_____

Today, I am (was) grateful for:

_____

_____

_____

March 28

"The universe is not punishing you or blessing you. The universe is responding to the vibrational attitude you are emitting."

– Abraham Hicks

MORNING

My intention for today is:

_____

_____

_____

NIGHTTIME

The high point of my day was:

_____

_____

_____

The low point of my day was:

_____

_____

_____

Today, I am (was) grateful for:

_____

_____

_____

March 29

"Awakened living is a recognition that the basis of life is freedom and the purpose of life is joy."

— TJ Woodward

MORNING

My intention for today is:

_____

_____

_____

NIGHTTIME

The high point of my day was:

_____

_____

_____

The low point of my day was:

_____

_____

_____

Today, I am (was) grateful for:

_____

_____

_____

March 30

*"Darkness cannot drive out darkness; only light can do that.
Hate cannot drive out hate; only love can do that."*
— Martin Luther King Jr.

MORNING

My intention for today is:

_____

_____

_____

NIGHTTIME

The high point of my day was:

_____

_____

_____

The low point of my day was:

_____

_____

_____

Today, I am (was) grateful for:

_____

_____

_____

March 31

"When we awaken, we no longer make ourselves victims to anyone's behavior, and we no longer blame ourselves or others."
– TJ Woodward

MORNING

My intention for today is:

_____
_____
_____

NIGHTTIME

The high point of my day was:

_____
_____
_____

The low point of my day was:

_____
_____
_____

Today, I am (was) grateful for:

_____
_____
_____

April 1

"Peace and happiness are both states of being in the world.
They are choices."

— TJ Woodward

MORNING

My intention for today is:

_____

_____

_____

NIGHTTIME

The high point of my day was:

_____

_____

_____

The low point of my day was:

_____

_____

_____

Today, I am (was) grateful for:

_____

_____

_____

April 2

"We don't see things the way they are.
We see things the way WE are."

– The Talmud

MORNING

My intention for today is:

_____

_____

_____

NIGHTTIME

The high point of my day was:

_____

_____

_____

The low point of my day was:

_____

_____

_____

Today, I am (was) grateful for:

_____

_____

_____

April 3

"Sometimes things need to break down so you can accept a larger vision for your life."

— TJ Woodward

MORNING

My intention for today is:

_____

_____

_____

NIGHTTIME

The high point of my day was:

_____

_____

_____

The low point of my day was:

_____

_____

_____

Today, I am (was) grateful for:

_____

_____

_____

April 4

*"The whole world can love you, but that won't make you happy.
What will make you happy is the love coming out of you."*

– Don Miguel Ruiz

MORNING

My intention for today is:

_____

_____

_____

NIGHTTIME

The high point of my day was:

_____

_____

_____

The low point of my day was:

_____

_____

_____

Today, I am (was) grateful for:

_____

_____

_____

April 5

"Happiness is a state of contentment
and satisfaction with what is."

– TJ Woodward

MORNING

My intention for today is:

_____

_____

_____

NIGHTTIME

The high point of my day was:

_____

_____

_____

The low point of my day was:

_____

_____

_____

Today, I am (was) grateful for:

_____

_____

_____

April 6

"There comes a point in life when we must take responsibility for our own well-being, instead of giving the power to others."

— Unknown

MORNING

My intention for today is:

_____

_____

_____

NIGHTTIME

The high point of my day was:

_____

_____

_____

The low point of my day was:

_____

_____

_____

Today, I am (was) grateful for:

_____

_____

_____

April 7

*"An outer search for connection does not bring
the kind of love that heals."*

– TJ Woodward

MORNING

My intention for today is:

_____

_____

_____

NIGHTTIME

The high point of my day was:

_____

_____

_____

The low point of my day was:

_____

_____

_____

Today, I am (was) grateful for:

_____

_____

_____

April 8

"Life is hard and learning is painful –
until it isn't."

– Dr. Sue Morter

MORNING

My intention for today is:

_____

_____

_____

NIGHTTIME

The high point of my day was:

_____

_____

_____

The low point of my day was:

_____

_____

_____

Today, I am (was) grateful for:

_____

_____

_____

April 9

*"When you've undergone a quantum shift in consciousness,
you will be more aware of the natural rhythm of life."*

– TJ Woodward

MORNING

My intention for today is:

_____

_____

_____

NIGHTTIME

The high point of my day was:

_____

_____

_____

The low point of my day was:

_____

_____

_____

Today, I am (was) grateful for:

_____

_____

_____

April 10

"Do not be dismayed by the brokenness of the world.
All things break. And all things are mended."

— L.R. Knost

MORNING

My intention for today is:

_____

_____

_____

NIGHTTIME

The high point of my day was:

_____

_____

_____

The low point of my day was:

_____

_____

_____

Today, I am (was) grateful for:

_____

_____

_____

April 11

"We can decide that no matter what happens, we are going to remain open-hearted, loving, and connected."
— TJ Woodward

MORNING

My intention for today is:

_____

_____

_____

NIGHTTIME

The high point of my day was:

_____

_____

_____

The low point of my day was:

_____

_____

_____

Today, I am (was) grateful for:

_____

_____

_____

April 12

"The future is a concept, it doesn't exist. There is no such thing as tomorrow. There never will be because time is always now."

– Alan Watts

MORNING

My intention for today is:

_____

_____

_____

NIGHTTIME

The high point of my day was:

_____

_____

_____

The low point of my day was:

_____

_____

_____

Today, I am (was) grateful for:

_____

_____

_____

April 13

"Even amidst the most dire circumstances, you can consciously create the life of your dreams."

— TJ Woodward

MORNING

My intention for today is:

_____

_____

_____

NIGHTTIME

The high point of my day was:

_____

_____

_____

The low point of my day was:

_____

_____

_____

Today, I am (was) grateful for:

_____

_____

_____

April 14

"I think everybody should get rich and famous and do everything they ever dreamed of so they can see that it's not the answer."
— Jim Carrey

MORNING

My intention for today is:

_____

_____

_____

NIGHTTIME

The high point of my day was:

_____

_____

_____

The low point of my day was:

_____

_____

_____

Today, I am (was) grateful for:

_____

_____

_____

April 15

"If you haven't examined your unconscious assumptions, they are running the show and making choices for you."

— TJ Woodward

MORNING

My intention for today is:

_____

_____

_____

NIGHTTIME

The high point of my day was:

_____

_____

_____

The low point of my day was:

_____

_____

_____

Today, I am (was) grateful for:

_____

_____

_____

April 16

*"The sole purpose of human existence is to kindle a
light in the darkness of mere being."*

– Carl Jung

MORNING

My intention for today is:

_____

_____

_____

NIGHTTIME

The high point of my day was:

_____

_____

_____

The low point of my day was:

_____

_____

_____

Today, I am (was) grateful for:

_____

_____

_____

April 17

"A deep relationship with your essential self is what brings true peace and happiness."

– TJ Woodward

MORNING

My intention for today is:

_____

_____

_____

NIGHTTIME

The high point of my day was:

_____

_____

_____

The low point of my day was:

_____

_____

_____

Today, I am (was) grateful for:

_____

_____

_____

April 18

"All our theories of improving the world, while we are still asleep, merely intensify the sleep of humanity."

– Maurice Nicoll

MORNING

My intention for today is:

_____

_____

_____

NIGHTTIME

The high point of my day was:

_____

_____

_____

The low point of my day was:

_____

_____

_____

Today, I am (was) grateful for:

_____

_____

_____

April 19

*"The spiritual journey is not about eradicating
perceived difficult life situations."*

— TJ Woodward

MORNING

My intention for today is:

_____

_____

_____

NIGHTTIME

The high point of my day was:

_____

_____

_____

The low point of my day was:

_____

_____

_____

Today, I am (was) grateful for:

_____

_____

_____

April 20

*"My speaking is intended to shake you awake,
not tell you how to dream better."*

– Adyashanti

MORNING

My intention for today is:

_____

_____

_____

NIGHTTIME

The high point of my day was:

_____

_____

_____

The low point of my day was:

_____

_____

_____

Today, I am (was) grateful for:

_____

_____

_____

April 21

"The more we live as love, the more positive impact we have on people around us and the world at large."

— TJ Woodward

MORNING

My intention for today is:

_____

_____

_____

NIGHTTIME

The high point of my day was:

_____

_____

_____

The low point of my day was:

_____

_____

_____

Today, I am (was) grateful for:

_____

_____

_____

April 22

"I am created by love in every second. We all are, as the planets and the stars. So, what is there to fear?"

– Oriah Mountain Dreamer

MORNING

My intention for today is:

_____

_____

_____

NIGHTTIME

The high point of my day was:

_____

_____

_____

The low point of my day was:

_____

_____

_____

Today, I am (was) grateful for:

_____

_____

_____

April 23

"Asking the question" 'What wants to be born here?'
can assist us in times of uncertainty."

— TJ Woodward

MORNING

My intention for today is:

_____

_____

_____

NIGHTTIME

The high point of my day was:

_____

_____

_____

The low point of my day was:

_____

_____

_____

Today, I am (was) grateful for:

_____

_____

_____

April 24

*"Letting go can be challenging, but
holding on can be even harder."*

– Unknown

MORNING

My intention for today is:

_____

_____

_____

NIGHTTIME

The high point of my day was:

_____

_____

_____

The low point of my day was:

_____

_____

_____

Today, I am (was) grateful for:

_____

_____

_____

April 25

"When we awaken to our true nature, we experience happiness in a very different way. We know it's a choice."

– TJ Woodward

MORNING

My intention for today is:

_____

_____

_____

NIGHTTIME

The high point of my day was:

_____

_____

_____

The low point of my day was:

_____

_____

_____

Today, I am (was) grateful for:

_____

_____

_____

April 26

"Every single judgment you tell yourself was not there when you were born."

– Don Miguel Ruiz

MORNING

My intention for today is:

_____

_____

_____

NIGHTTIME

The high point of my day was:

_____

_____

_____

The low point of my day was:

_____

_____

_____

Today, I am (was) grateful for:

_____

_____

_____

April 27

*"Awakened living is experiencing life through the lens
of curiosity, awe, and wonder."*

— TJ Woodward

MORNING

My intention for today is:

_____

_____

_____

NIGHTTIME

The high point of my day was:

_____

_____

_____

The low point of my day was:

_____

_____

_____

Today, I am (was) grateful for:

_____

_____

_____

April 28

"Once you realize that all comes from within, and that the world in which you live is projected by you, fear comes to an end."
— Nisargaradatta Maharaj

MORNING

My intention for today is:

_____

_____

_____

NIGHTTIME

The high point of my day was:

_____

_____

_____

The low point of my day was:

_____

_____

_____

Today, I am (was) grateful for:

_____

_____

_____

April 29

"When we surrender to our inner source, we discover it is stronger than any external force we can imagine."

— TJ Woodward

MORNING

My intention for today is:

_____

_____

_____

NIGHTTIME

The high point of my day was:

_____

_____

_____

The low point of my day was:

_____

_____

_____

Today, I am (was) grateful for:

_____

_____

_____

April 30

"Wisdom is knowing I am nothing, love is knowing I am everything, and between the two my life moves."

– The Dalai Lama

MORNING

My intention for today is:

_____

_____

_____

NIGHTTIME

The high point of my day was:

_____

_____

_____

The low point of my day was:

_____

_____

_____

Today, I am (was) grateful for:

_____

_____

_____

May 1

"The frequency at which we are vibrating, and the energy we're holding, creates what we call reality."

— TJ Woodward

MORNING

My intention for today is:

_____

_____

_____

NIGHTTIME

The high point of my day was:

_____

_____

_____

The low point of my day was:

_____

_____

_____

Today, I am (was) grateful for:

_____

_____

_____

May 2

*"You are never given a wish without also being given the power
to make it come true. You may have to work for it, however."*

– Unknown

MORNING

My intention for today is:

_____

_____

_____

NIGHTTIME

The high point of my day was:

_____

_____

_____

The low point of my day was:

_____

_____

_____

Today, I am (was) grateful for:

_____

_____

_____

May 3

*"Addictive behavior is a strategy to unlearn
rather than a problem to solve."*

– TJ Woodward

MORNING

My intention for today is:

_____

_____

_____

NIGHTTIME

The high point of my day was:

_____

_____

_____

The low point of my day was:

_____

_____

_____

Today, I am (was) grateful for:

_____

_____

_____

May 4

"The song of your soul is longing to be sung.
Let your own essence express itself freely."

– Brandon Bays

MORNING

My intention for today is:

_____

_____

_____

NIGHTTIME

The high point of my day was:

_____

_____

_____

The low point of my day was:

_____

_____

_____

Today, I am (was) grateful for:

_____

_____

_____

May 5

*"Practicing spiritual principles allows you to unlearn
habits of judgment and resistance."*

– TJ Woodward

MORNING

My intention for today is:

_____

_____

_____

NIGHTTIME

The high point of my day was:

_____

_____

_____

The low point of my day was:

_____

_____

_____

Today, I am (was) grateful for:

_____

_____

_____

May 6

*"By not accepting personal responsibility for our circumstances,
we greatly reduce our power to change them."*

– Steve Maraboli

MORNING

My intention for today is:

_____

_____

_____

NIGHTTIME

The high point of my day was:

_____

_____

_____

The low point of my day was:

_____

_____

_____

Today, I am (was) grateful for:

_____

_____

_____

May 7

"As you identify and overcome limiting inner constructs, infinite possibilities open to you."

– TJ Woodward

MORNING

My intention for today is:

_____

_____

_____

NIGHTTIME

The high point of my day was:

_____

_____

_____

The low point of my day was:

_____

_____

_____

Today, I am (was) grateful for:

_____

_____

_____

May 8

*"Be thankful for what you have, you'll end up having more.
Focus on what you don't have, you will never have enough."*
— Oprah Winfrey

MORNING

My intention for today is:

_____

_____

_____

NIGHTTIME

The high point of my day was:

_____

_____

_____

The low point of my day was:

_____

_____

_____

Today, I am (was) grateful for:

_____

_____

_____

May 9

*"Growing in awareness of who and what you truly
are is your fundamental purpose."*

– TJ Woodward

MORNING

My intention for today is:

_____

_____

_____

NIGHTTIME

The high point of my day was:

_____

_____

_____

The low point of my day was:

_____

_____

_____

Today, I am (was) grateful for:

_____

_____

_____

May 10

"If an egg is broken from the outside, life ends. If an egg is broken from the inside, life begins. Great things happen inside."
– Unknown

MORNING

My intention for today is:

_____

_____

_____

NIGHTTIME

The high point of my day was:

_____

_____

_____

The low point of my day was:

_____

_____

_____

Today, I am (was) grateful for:

_____

_____

_____

May 11

*"When we truly recognize our oneness with spirit, we live
beyond judgment of ourselves and others."*

— TJ Woodward

MORNING

My intention for today is:

_____

_____

_____

NIGHTTIME

The high point of my day was:

_____

_____

_____

The low point of my day was:

_____

_____

_____

Today, I am (was) grateful for:

_____

_____

_____

May 12

"Every thought, every action, creates ripples through this infinite field of consciousness."

– Unknown

MORNING

My intention for today is:

_____

_____

_____

NIGHTTIME

The high point of my day was:

_____

_____

_____

The low point of my day was:

_____

_____

_____

Today, I am (was) grateful for:

_____

_____

_____

May 13

"Awakened living is waking up from the illusion of separation, fear, and scarcity, and returning to our original perfection."

— TJ Woodward

MORNING

My intention for today is:

_____

_____

_____

NIGHTTIME

The high point of my day was:

_____

_____

_____

The low point of my day was:

_____

_____

_____

Today, I am (was) grateful for:

_____

_____

_____

May 14

*"Be brave enough to
start a conversation that matters."*

— Unknown

MORNING

My intention for today is:

_____

_____

_____

NIGHTTIME

The high point of my day was:

_____

_____

_____

The low point of my day was:

_____

_____

_____

Today, I am (was) grateful for:

_____

_____

_____

May 15

"As we awaken, we realize that life is not happening to us,
it is happening through us, and as us."

— TJ Woodward

MORNING

My intention for today is:

_____

_____

_____

NIGHTTIME

The high point of my day was:

_____

_____

_____

The low point of my day was:

_____

_____

_____

Today, I am (was) grateful for:

_____

_____

_____

May 16

"Compassion is not a relationship between the healer and the wounded. It's a relationship between equals."

– Pema Chodron

MORNING

My intention for today is:

_____

_____

_____

NIGHTTIME

The high point of my day was:

_____

_____

_____

The low point of my day was:

_____

_____

_____

Today, I am (was) grateful for:

_____

_____

_____

May 17

"Living an awakened life is living beyond your stories of shame and trauma. It's living in a state of openness and curiosity."

— TJ Woodward

MORNING

My intention for today is:

_____

_____

_____

NIGHTTIME

The high point of my day was:

_____

_____

_____

The low point of my day was:

_____

_____

_____

Today, I am (was) grateful for:

_____

_____

_____

May 18

*"All it takes is one person in any generation
to heal a family's limiting beliefs."*

— Gregg Braden

MORNING

My intention for today is:

_____

_____

_____

NIGHTTIME

The high point of my day was:

_____

_____

_____

The low point of my day was:

_____

_____

_____

Today, I am (was) grateful for:

_____

_____

_____

May 19

"When we 'unlearn' and remember who we truly are, we are no longer bound by the events in our past."

— TJ Woodward

MORNING

My intention for today is:

_____

_____

_____

NIGHTTIME

The high point of my day was:

_____

_____

_____

The low point of my day was:

_____

_____

_____

Today, I am (was) grateful for:

_____

_____

_____

May 20

*"When you forgive, you in no way change the past,
but you sure do change the future."*

– Bernard Meltzer

MORNING

My intention for today is:

_____

_____

_____

NIGHTTIME

The high point of my day was:

_____

_____

_____

The low point of my day was:

_____

_____

_____

Today, I am (was) grateful for:

_____

_____

_____

May 21

"We come into this world as spiritual beings intuitively experiencing our oneness with source energy."

— TJ Woodward

MORNING

My intention for today is:

_____

_____

_____

NIGHTTIME

The high point of my day was:

_____

_____

_____

The low point of my day was:

_____

_____

_____

Today, I am (was) grateful for:

_____

_____

_____

May 22

*"The desire to know your own soul
will end all other desires."*

– Rumi

MORNING

My intention for today is:

_____

_____

_____

NIGHTTIME

The high point of my day was:

_____

_____

_____

The low point of my day was:

_____

_____

_____

Today, I am (was) grateful for:

_____

_____

_____

May 23

"I am whole and perfect in every way. From a spiritual perspective, life's journey is an attempt to reclaim this truth."
— TJ Woodward

MORNING

My intention for today is:

_____

_____

_____

NIGHTTIME

The high point of my day was:

_____

_____

_____

The low point of my day was:

_____

_____

_____

Today, I am (was) grateful for:

_____

_____

_____

May 24

"I did not come to teach you. I came to love you.
Love will teach you."

— Unknown

MORNING

My intention for today is:

_____

_____

_____

NIGHTTIME

The high point of my day was:

_____

_____

_____

The low point of my day was:

_____

_____

_____

Today, I am (was) grateful for:

_____

_____

_____

May 25

"Walking around with unresolved psychic pain is a root cause of addictive tendencies."

— TJ Woodward

MORNING

My intention for today is:

_____

_____

_____

NIGHTTIME

The high point of my day was:

_____

_____

_____

The low point of my day was:

_____

_____

_____

Today, I am (was) grateful for:

_____

_____

_____

May 26

*"Why continue rehearsing the role of a victim
when you could be free and happy?"*

– Gabrielle Bernstein

MORNING

My intention for today is:

_____

_____

_____

NIGHTTIME

The high point of my day was:

_____

_____

_____

The low point of my day was:

_____

_____

_____

Today, I am (was) grateful for:

_____

_____

_____

May 27

"When we learn to flow with life rather than resisting it, we enter into a life filled with love, gratitude, and joy."

— TJ Woodward

MORNING

My intention for today is:

_____

_____

_____

NIGHTTIME

The high point of my day was:

_____

_____

_____

The low point of my day was:

_____

_____

_____

Today, I am (was) grateful for:

_____

_____

_____

May 28

"What most people need to learn in life is how to love people and use things, instead of using people and loving things."

– Unknown

MORNING

My intention for today is:

_____

_____

_____

NIGHTTIME

The high point of my day was:

_____

_____

_____

The low point of my day was:

_____

_____

_____

Today, I am (was) grateful for:

_____

_____

_____

May 29

*"Each of us waking up has a ripple effect on the collective;
on politics, on the health of the planet, on everything."*
— TJ Woodward

MORNING

My intention for today is:

_____

_____

_____

NIGHTTIME

The high point of my day was:

_____

_____

_____

The low point of my day was:

_____

_____

_____

Today, I am (was) grateful for:

_____

_____

_____

May 30

*"Often it's the deepest pain that empowers you
to grow into your highest self."*

– Karen Salmansohn

MORNING

My intention for today is:

_____

_____

_____

NIGHTTIME

The high point of my day was:

_____

_____

_____

The low point of my day was:

_____

_____

_____

Today, I am (was) grateful for:

_____

_____

_____

May 31

"Victim consciousness leaves us feeling powerless over circumstances. This viewpoint offers us little choice."

— TJ Woodward

MORNING

My intention for today is:

_____

_____

_____

NIGHTTIME

The high point of my day was:

_____

_____

_____

The low point of my day was:

_____

_____

_____

Today, I am (was) grateful for:

_____

_____

_____

June 1

"What is often at the core of addictive behavior is a sense of brokenness within and an outer search for comfort."
— TJ Woodward

MORNING

My intention for today is:

_____

_____

_____

NIGHTTIME

The high point of my day was:

_____

_____

_____

The low point of my day was:

_____

_____

_____

Today, I am (was) grateful for:

_____

_____

_____

June 2

"Ego tries to convince us that we must 'do' in order to achieve.
Spirit knows life is a magnificent consequence of being."

– Dean Jackson

MORNING

My intention for today is:

_____

_____

_____

NIGHTTIME

The high point of my day was:

_____

_____

_____

The low point of my day was:

_____

_____

_____

Today, I am (was) grateful for:

_____

_____

_____

June 3

"If we have a core belief that the world is not safe we tend to develop strategies for making this belief more bearable."
— TJ Woodward

MORNING

My intention for today is:

_____

_____

_____

NIGHTTIME

The high point of my day was:

_____

_____

_____

The low point of my day was:

_____

_____

_____

Today, I am (was) grateful for:

_____

_____

_____

June 4

*"I choose to make the rest of my life
the best of my life."*

– Louise Hay

MORNING

My intention for today is:

_____

_____

_____

NIGHTTIME

The high point of my day was:

_____

_____

_____

The low point of my day was:

_____

_____

_____

Today, I am (was) grateful for:

_____

_____

_____

June 5

*"We don't call it an addiction as long as it is working;
we call it fun."*

— TJ Woodward

MORNING

My intention for today is:

_____

_____

_____

NIGHTTIME

The high point of my day was:

_____

_____

_____

The low point of my day was:

_____

_____

_____

Today, I am (was) grateful for:

_____

_____

_____

June 6

*"Every accomplishment starts
with the decision to try."*

– Gail Devers

MORNING

My intention for today is:

_____

_____

_____

NIGHTTIME

The high point of my day was:

_____

_____

_____

The low point of my day was:

_____

_____

_____

Today, I am (was) grateful for:

_____

_____

_____

June 7

"Patience will help you open to what the recovery process is wanting to reveal."

– TJ Woodward

MORNING

My intention for today is:

_____

_____

_____

NIGHTTIME

The high point of my day was:

_____

_____

_____

The low point of my day was:

_____

_____

_____

Today, I am (was) grateful for:

_____

_____

_____

June 8

"What we have learned to look for in a situation determines mostly what we see."

– Ellen Langer

MORNING

My intention for today is:

_____

_____

_____

NIGHTTIME

The high point of my day was:

_____

_____

_____

The low point of my day was:

_____

_____

_____

Today, I am (was) grateful for:

_____

_____

_____

June 9

"Toxic shame thrives in an environment where people are not seen for who they are."

– TJ Woodward

MORNING

My intention for today is:

_____

_____

_____

NIGHTTIME

The high point of my day was:

_____

_____

_____

The low point of my day was:

_____

_____

_____

Today, I am (was) grateful for:

_____

_____

_____

June 10

*"The only Zen you find at the top of the mountain
is the Zen you bring with you."*

— Zen Proverb

MORNING

My intention for today is:

_____

_____

_____

NIGHTTIME

The high point of my day was:

_____

_____

_____

The low point of my day was:

_____

_____

_____

Today, I am (was) grateful for:

_____

_____

_____

June 11

*"Releasing our dependence on old emotional patterns
is a major component of recovery."*

– TJ Woodward

MORNING

My intention for today is:

_____

_____

_____

NIGHTTIME

The high point of my day was:

_____

_____

_____

The low point of my day was:

_____

_____

_____

Today, I am (was) grateful for:

_____

_____

_____

June 12

"The human soul doesn't want to be advised or fixed or saved.
It simply wants to be witnessed…exactly as it is."

– Parker Palmer

MORNING

My intention for today is:

_____

_____

_____

NIGHTTIME

The high point of my day was:

_____

_____

_____

The low point of my day was:

_____

_____

_____

Today, I am (was) grateful for:

_____

_____

_____

June 13

"People with toxic shame unconsciously long for brokenness
in other people and situations."

— TJ Woodward

MORNING

My intention for today is:

_____

_____

_____

NIGHTTIME

The high point of my day was:

_____

_____

_____

The low point of my day was:

_____

_____

_____

Today, I am (was) grateful for:

_____

_____

_____

June 14

"The best time to plant a tree was twenty years ago.
The second best time is now."

— Chinese Proverb

MORNING

My intention for today is:

_____

_____

_____

NIGHTTIME

The high point of my day was:

_____

_____

_____

The low point of my day was:

_____

_____

_____

Today, I am (was) grateful for:

_____

_____

_____

June 15

"Love and acceptance are more powerful change agents than judgment and criticism."

– TJ Woodward

MORNING

My intention for today is:

_____

_____

_____

NIGHTTIME

The high point of my day was:

_____

_____

_____

The low point of my day was:

_____

_____

_____

Today, I am (was) grateful for:

_____

_____

_____

June 16

"We are so engrossed with the objects, or appearances revealed by the light, that we pay no attention to the light itself."
— Ramana Maharshi

MORNING

My intention for today is:

_____

_____

_____

NIGHTTIME

The high point of my day was:

_____

_____

_____

The low point of my day was:

_____

_____

_____

Today, I am (was) grateful for:

_____

_____

_____

June 17

*"Surrounding yourself with people who share a common
intention can be a powerful tool for transformation."*

– TJ Woodward

MORNING

My intention for today is:

_____

_____

_____

NIGHTTIME

The high point of my day was:

_____

_____

_____

The low point of my day was:

_____

_____

_____

Today, I am (was) grateful for:

_____

_____

_____

June 18

*"Those who have a 'why' to live
can bear almost any 'how.'"*

— Friedrich Nietzsche

MORNING

My intention for today is:

_____

_____

_____

NIGHTTIME

The high point of my day was:

_____

_____

_____

The low point of my day was:

_____

_____

_____

Today, I am (was) grateful for:

_____

_____

_____

June 19

"A root cause of suffering is clinging to the idea that things in the external world need to be a certain way."

— TJ Woodward

MORNING

My intention for today is:

_____

_____

_____

NIGHTTIME

The high point of my day was:

_____

_____

_____

The low point of my day was:

_____

_____

_____

Today, I am (was) grateful for:

_____

_____

_____

June 20

*"True meditation is sitting open to whatever is happening –
pleasant or unpleasant."*

– Adyashanti

MORNING

My intention for today is:

_____

_____

_____

NIGHTTIME

The high point of my day was:

_____

_____

_____

The low point of my day was:

_____

_____

_____

Today, I am (was) grateful for:

_____

_____

_____

June 21

"When we switch from 'I am depressed' to 'I feel depressed' a powerful shift occurs."

– TJ Woodward

MORNING

My intention for today is:

_____

_____

_____

NIGHTTIME

The high point of my day was:

_____

_____

_____

The low point of my day was:

_____

_____

_____

Today, I am (was) grateful for:

_____

_____

_____

June 22

"To live is the rarest thing in the world.
Most people exist, that is all."

– Oscar Wilde

MORNING

My intention for today is:

_____

_____

_____

NIGHTTIME

The high point of my day was:

_____

_____

_____

The low point of my day was:

_____

_____

_____

Today, I am (was) grateful for:

_____

_____

_____

June 23

*"We tend to experience the world as broken
if we believe we are broken."*

– TJ Woodward

MORNING

My intention for today is:

_____

_____

_____

NIGHTTIME

The high point of my day was:

_____

_____

_____

The low point of my day was:

_____

_____

_____

Today, I am (was) grateful for:

_____

_____

_____

June 24

*"Even death is not to be feared by
one who has lived wisely."*

— Unknown

MORNING

My intention for today is:

_____

_____

_____

NIGHTTIME

The high point of my day was:

_____

_____

_____

The low point of my day was:

_____

_____

_____

Today, I am (was) grateful for:

_____

_____

_____

June 25

"Simply said, addictive behavior is a response to the fear of being truly present with your emotions."

– TJ Woodward

MORNING

My intention for today is:

_____

_____

_____

NIGHTTIME

The high point of my day was:

_____

_____

_____

The low point of my day was:

_____

_____

_____

Today, I am (was) grateful for:

_____

_____

_____

June 26

"A quiet mind married to integrity of heart is the birth of wisdom."

— Adyashanti

MORNING

My intention for today is:

_____

_____

_____

NIGHTTIME

The high point of my day was:

_____

_____

_____

The low point of my day was:

_____

_____

_____

Today, I am (was) grateful for:

_____

_____

_____

June 27

"Magnificent new paradigms are often doubted by the masses before a major shift occurs."

— TJ Woodward

MORNING

My intention for today is:

_____

_____

_____

NIGHTTIME

The high point of my day was:

_____

_____

_____

The low point of my day was:

_____

_____

_____

Today, I am (was) grateful for:

_____

_____

_____

June 28

*"All things in this vast universe exist
within you and for you."*

— Kahlil Gibran

MORNING

My intention for today is:

_____

_____

_____

NIGHTTIME

The high point of my day was:

_____

_____

_____

The low point of my day was:

_____

_____

_____

Today, I am (was) grateful for:

_____

_____

_____

June 29

"When we are not awake to our true nature, we can be easily triggered by the words and behavior of others."

– TJ Woodward

MORNING

My intention for today is:

_____
_____
_____

NIGHTTIME

The high point of my day was:

_____
_____
_____

The low point of my day was:

_____
_____
_____

Today, I am (was) grateful for:

_____
_____
_____

June 30

*"Nothing can trouble you but
your own imagination."*

— Misargadatta Maharaj

MORNING

My intention for today is:

_____

_____

_____

NIGHTTIME

The high point of my day was:

_____

_____

_____

The low point of my day was:

_____

_____

_____

Today, I am (was) grateful for:

_____

_____

_____

July 1

"It is not helpful to ask our minds to stop seeking answers.
That is like telling the heart to stop pumping blood."

— TJ Woodward

MORNING

My intention for today is:

_____

_____

_____

NIGHTTIME

The high point of my day was:

_____

_____

_____

The low point of my day was:

_____

_____

_____

Today, I am (was) grateful for:

_____

_____

_____

July 2

"A scholar tries to learn something daily; a student of Buddhism tries to unlearn something daily."

— Alan Watts

MORNING

My intention for today is:

_____

_____

_____

NIGHTTIME

The high point of my day was:

_____

_____

_____

The low point of my day was:

_____

_____

_____

Today, I am (was) grateful for:

_____

_____

_____

July 3

"Consciously creating your life involves unearthing what lies in the shadow; the beliefs you've unconsciously created.
— TJ Woodward

MORNING

My intention for today is:

_____

_____

_____

NIGHTTIME

The high point of my day was:

_____

_____

_____

The low point of my day was:

_____

_____

_____

Today, I am (was) grateful for:

_____

_____

_____

July 4

"Challenge your unexamined beliefs. No longer be imprisoned by your own ignorance. Freedom is found in self-awareness."

– Zen Thinking

MORNING

My intention for today is:

_____

_____

_____

NIGHTTIME

The high point of my day was:

_____

_____

_____

The low point of my day was:

_____

_____

_____

Today, I am (was) grateful for:

_____

_____

_____

July 5

"If we only change things on the outside we are just 'rearranging the deck chairs on the Titanic' as the saying goes."

– TJ Woodward

MORNING

My intention for today is:

_____

_____

_____

NIGHTTIME

The high point of my day was:

_____

_____

_____

The low point of my day was:

_____

_____

_____

Today, I am (was) grateful for:

_____

_____

_____

July 6

"Happiness is a choice, not a result. Your happiness will not come to you. It can only come from you."

— Unknown

MORNING

My intention for today is:

_____

_____

_____

NIGHTTIME

The high point of my day was:

_____

_____

_____

The low point of my day was:

_____

_____

_____

Today, I am (was) grateful for:

_____

_____

_____

July 7

"Deepening your spiritual practice will open you to more love, connection, and happiness than you've ever known."

— TJ Woodward

MORNING

My intention for today is:

_____

_____

_____

NIGHTTIME

The high point of my day was:

_____

_____

_____

The low point of my day was:

_____

_____

_____

Today, I am (was) grateful for:

_____

_____

_____

July 8

"Many times what people need is not a brilliant mind that speaks, but a special heart that listens."

– Unknown

MORNING

My intention for today is:

_____

_____

_____

NIGHTTIME

The high point of my day was:

_____

_____

_____

The low point of my day was:

_____

_____

_____

Today, I am (was) grateful for:

_____

_____

_____

July 9

*"Shifts that come by only changing our thoughts
will likely be, at best, temporary."*

– TJ Woodward

MORNING

My intention for today is:

_____

_____

_____

NIGHTTIME

The high point of my day was:

_____

_____

_____

The low point of my day was:

_____

_____

_____

Today, I am (was) grateful for:

_____

_____

_____

July 10

"There is no more powerful source of creative energy in the world than a turned-on, empowered human being."

— John Mackey

MORNING

My intention for today is:

_____

_____

_____

NIGHTTIME

The high point of my day was:

_____

_____

_____

The low point of my day was:

_____

_____

_____

Today, I am (was) grateful for:

_____

_____

_____

July 11

*"You can only accept and step into the life
you believe you deserve."*

– TJ Woodward

MORNING

My intention for today is:

_____

_____

_____

NIGHTTIME

The high point of my day was:

_____

_____

_____

The low point of my day was:

_____

_____

_____

Today, I am (was) grateful for:

_____

_____

_____

July 12

"Watch for the people whose eyes light up when you talk about your dream. Those are the people you keep."

– Elizabeth Gilbert

MORNING

My intention for today is:

_____

_____

_____

NIGHTTIME

The high point of my day was:

_____

_____

_____

The low point of my day was:

_____

_____

_____

Today, I am (was) grateful for:

_____

_____

_____

July 13

"Something powerful happens when we shift our focus from what we DON'T want to what we DO want."

– TJ Woodward

MORNING

My intention for today is:

_____

_____

_____

NIGHTTIME

The high point of my day was:

_____

_____

_____

The low point of my day was:

_____

_____

_____

Today, I am (was) grateful for:

_____

_____

_____

July 14

"Through early programming, we look for approval outside ourselves rather than inwardly satisfying our own creativity."

– Temple Hayes

MORNING

My intention for today is:

_____

_____

_____

NIGHTTIME

The high point of my day was:

_____

_____

_____

The low point of my day was:

_____

_____

_____

Today, I am (was) grateful for:

_____

_____

_____

July 15

"Most obstacles we encounter reside within. They come from feeling that we don't deserve the life we desire."

– TJ Woodward

MORNING

My intention for today is:

_____

_____

_____

NIGHTTIME

The high point of my day was:

_____

_____

_____

The low point of my day was:

_____

_____

_____

Today, I am (was) grateful for:

_____

_____

_____

July 16

"Let your light shine. Shine within you so that it can shine on someone else. Let your light shine."

— Oprah Winfrey

MORNING

My intention for today is:

_____

_____

_____

NIGHTTIME

The high point of my day was:

_____

_____

_____

The low point of my day was:

_____

_____

_____

Today, I am (was) grateful for:

_____

_____

_____

July 17

"Making peace with the adverse stories you've created unconsciously will allow your genuine dreams to emerge."
— TJ Woodward

MORNING

My intention for today is:

_____

_____

_____

NIGHTTIME

The high point of my day was:

_____

_____

_____

The low point of my day was:

_____

_____

_____

Today, I am (was) grateful for:

_____

_____

_____

July 18

"Our goal while on this earth is to transcend our illusions and discover the innate power of our spirit."

– Caroline Myss

MORNING

My intention for today is:

_____

_____

_____

NIGHTTIME

The high point of my day was:

_____

_____

_____

The low point of my day was:

_____

_____

_____

Today, I am (was) grateful for:

_____

_____

_____

July 19

"When we are no longer overly identified with our minds, we can access the wisdom of our emotional inner landscape."

— TJ Woodward

MORNING

My intention for today is:

_____

_____

_____

NIGHTTIME

The high point of my day was:

_____

_____

_____

The low point of my day was:

_____

_____

_____

Today, I am (was) grateful for:

_____

_____

_____

July 20

"Until one has loved an animal a part of one's soul remains unawakened."

— Anatole France

MORNING

My intention for today is:

_____

_____

_____

NIGHTTIME

The high point of my day was:

_____

_____

_____

The low point of my day was:

_____

_____

_____

Today, I am (was) grateful for:

_____

_____

_____

July 21

*"If you had a fresh canvas on which to paint your life,
what masterpiece would you create?"*

— TJ Woodward

MORNING

My intention for today is:

_____

_____

_____

NIGHTTIME

The high point of my day was:

_____

_____

_____

The low point of my day was:

_____

_____

_____

Today, I am (was) grateful for:

_____

_____

_____

July 22

"Successful people are just ordinary folks who have developed belief in themselves and what they do."
— David J. Schwartz

MORNING

My intention for today is:

_____

_____

_____

NIGHTTIME

The high point of my day was:

_____

_____

_____

The low point of my day was:

_____

_____

_____

Today, I am (was) grateful for:

_____

_____

_____

July 23

"Making peace with the past is the first step in consciously creating the life of your dreams."

— TJ Woodward

MORNING

My intention for today is:

_____

_____

_____

NIGHTTIME

The high point of my day was:

_____

_____

_____

The low point of my day was:

_____

_____

_____

Today, I am (was) grateful for:

_____

_____

_____

July 24

"The effect you have on others is the most
valuable currency there is."

– Jim Carrey

MORNING

My intention for today is:

_____

_____

_____

NIGHTTIME

The high point of my day was:

_____

_____

_____

The low point of my day was:

_____

_____

_____

Today, I am (was) grateful for:

_____

_____

_____

July 25

"You don't need to fight your inner critic; you can simply recognize it for what it is; a single thought among many."

— TJ Woodward

MORNING

My intention for today is:

_____

_____

_____

NIGHTTIME

The high point of my day was:

_____

_____

_____

The low point of my day was:

_____

_____

_____

Today, I am (was) grateful for:

_____

_____

_____

July 26

"Thank you universe for all the good things in my life I don't yet know about."

– Michael Beckwith

MORNING

My intention for today is:

_____

_____

_____

NIGHTTIME

The high point of my day was:

_____

_____

_____

The low point of my day was:

_____

_____

_____

Today, I am (was) grateful for:

_____

_____

_____

July 27

"Feeling your feelings and responding in a conscious way is distinctly different that having a feeling and reacting to it."

– TJ Woodward

MORNING

My intention for today is:

_____

_____

_____

NIGHTTIME

The high point of my day was:

_____

_____

_____

The low point of my day was:

_____

_____

_____

Today, I am (was) grateful for:

_____

_____

_____

July 28

*"Being at ease with not knowing is crucial
for answers to come to you."*

— Eckhart Tolle

MORNING

My intention for today is:

_____

_____

_____

NIGHTTIME

The high point of my day was:

_____

_____

_____

The low point of my day was:

_____

_____

_____

Today, I am (was) grateful for:

_____

_____

_____

July 29

"Love, light, and divinity have always been the ultimate truth of who and what you are."

– TJ Woodward

MORNING

My intention for today is:

_____

_____

_____

NIGHTTIME

The high point of my day was:

_____

_____

_____

The low point of my day was:

_____

_____

_____

Today, I am (was) grateful for:

_____

_____

_____

July 30

"We are never more than a belief away from our greatest love, deepest healing, and most profound miracle."

– Gregg Braden

MORNING

My intention for today is:

_____

_____

_____

NIGHTTIME

The high point of my day was:

_____

_____

_____

The low point of my day was:

_____

_____

_____

Today, I am (was) grateful for:

_____

_____

_____

July 31

"We don't need to attract anything, because we already are everything. We are already whole and complete."
— TJ Woodward

MORNING

My intention for today is:

_____

_____

_____

NIGHTTIME

The high point of my day was:

_____

_____

_____

The low point of my day was:

_____

_____

_____

Today, I am (was) grateful for:

_____

_____

_____

August 1

"When we are out of touch with our wholeness, we believe we need to acquire something outside of us to be complete."
— TJ Woodward

MORNING

My intention for today is:

_____

_____

_____

NIGHTTIME

The high point of my day was:

_____

_____

_____

The low point of my day was:

_____

_____

_____

Today, I am (was) grateful for:

_____

_____

_____

August 2

"This is the secret of life – to be completely engaged with what you are doing now, and realize it's not work. It's play."

— Alan Watts

MORNING

My intention for today is:

_____

_____

_____

NIGHTTIME

The high point of my day was:

_____

_____

_____

The low point of my day was:

_____

_____

_____

Today, I am (was) grateful for:

_____

_____

_____

August 3

"Even in the midst of the seemingly unforgivable,
we can experience peace."

— TJ Woodward

MORNING

My intention for today is:

_____

_____

_____

NIGHTTIME

The high point of my day was:

_____

_____

_____

The low point of my day was:

_____

_____

_____

Today, I am (was) grateful for:

_____

_____

_____

August 4

"Enlightenment, in the end, is nothing more than the natural state of being."

— Adyashanti

MORNING

My intention for today is:

_____

_____

_____

NIGHTTIME

The high point of my day was:

_____

_____

_____

The low point of my day was:

_____

_____

_____

Today, I am (was) grateful for:

_____

_____

_____

August 5

"We won't be able to create our true story if we are continually recreating our false story."

— TJ Woodward

MORNING

My intention for today is:

_____

_____

_____

NIGHTTIME

The high point of my day was:

_____

_____

_____

The low point of my day was:

_____

_____

_____

Today, I am (was) grateful for:

_____

_____

_____

August 6

"Even a mistake may turn out to be the one thing necessary for a worthwhile achievement."

– Henry Ford

MORNING

My intention for today is:

_____

_____

_____

NIGHTTIME

The high point of my day was:

_____

_____

_____

The low point of my day was:

_____

_____

_____

Today, I am (was) grateful for:

_____

_____

_____

August 7

"As we develop spiritually, we begin to shift from the 'law of attraction' to the 'law of radiance.'"

— TJ Woodward

MORNING

My intention for today is:

_____

_____

_____

NIGHTTIME

The high point of my day was:

_____

_____

_____

The low point of my day was:

_____

_____

_____

Today, I am (was) grateful for:

_____

_____

_____

August 8

"What a caterpillar calls the end of the world,
we call a butterfly."

– Unknown

MORNING

My intention for today is:

_____

_____

_____

NIGHTTIME

The high point of my day was:

_____

_____

_____

The low point of my day was:

_____

_____

_____

Today, I am (was) grateful for:

_____

_____

_____

August 9

"When you're able to pause and witness your own thoughts,
it's one small step from self-criticism to self-compassion."

— TJ Woodward

MORNING

My intention for today is:

_____

_____

_____

NIGHTTIME

The high point of my day was:

_____

_____

_____

The low point of my day was:

_____

_____

_____

Today, I am (was) grateful for:

_____

_____

_____

August 10

"Trust the wait. Embrace the uncertainty. Enjoy the beauty of becoming. When nothing is known, anything is possible."

— Unknown

MORNING

My intention for today is:

_____

_____

_____

NIGHTTIME

The high point of my day was:

_____

_____

_____

The low point of my day was:

_____

_____

_____

Today, I am (was) grateful for:

_____

_____

_____

August 11

"We are the ones we've been waiting for. When we truly understand this, everything changes."

— TJ Woodward

MORNING

My intention for today is:

_____

_____

_____

NIGHTTIME

The high point of my day was:

_____

_____

_____

The low point of my day was:

_____

_____

_____

Today, I am (was) grateful for:

_____

_____

_____

August 12

"We can never obtain peace in the outer world
until we make peace with ourselves."

– Buddha

MORNING

My intention for today is:

_____

_____

_____

NIGHTTIME

The high point of my day was:

_____

_____

_____

The low point of my day was:

_____

_____

_____

Today, I am (was) grateful for:

_____

_____

_____

August 13

"It is impossible to truly forgive without a profound shift in consciousness."

– TJ Woodward

MORNING

My intention for today is:

_____

_____

_____

NIGHTTIME

The high point of my day was:

_____

_____

_____

The low point of my day was:

_____

_____

_____

Today, I am (was) grateful for:

_____

_____

_____

August 14

"The most beautiful things in the world cannot be seen or even touched. They must be felt with the heart."

— Helen Keller

MORNING

My intention for today is:

_____

_____

_____

NIGHTTIME

The high point of my day was:

_____

_____

_____

The low point of my day was:

_____

_____

_____

Today, I am (was) grateful for:

_____

_____

_____

August 15

"Conscious awareness is about making moment-to-moment decisions about where we place our focus."

— TJ Woodward

MORNING

My intention for today is:

_____

_____

_____

NIGHTTIME

The high point of my day was:

_____

_____

_____

The low point of my day was:

_____

_____

_____

Today, I am (was) grateful for:

_____

_____

_____

August 16

"There is no such thing as a simple act of compassion. Everything we do for another person has infinite consequences."

– Caroline Myss

MORNING

My intention for today is:

_____

_____

_____

NIGHTTIME

The high point of my day was:

_____

_____

_____

The low point of my day was:

_____

_____

_____

Today, I am (was) grateful for:

_____

_____

_____

August 17

"We might believe that ruminating on the past helps us change the future, but it usually only increases the story's power."
— TJ Woodward

MORNING

My intention for today is:

_____

_____

_____

NIGHTTIME

The high point of my day was:

_____

_____

_____

The low point of my day was:

_____

_____

_____

Today, I am (was) grateful for:

_____

_____

_____

August 18

*"You are always one decision away
from a totally different life."*

– Unknown

MORNING

My intention for today is:

_____

_____

_____

NIGHTTIME

The high point of my day was:

_____

_____

_____

The low point of my day was:

_____

_____

_____

Today, I am (was) grateful for:

_____

_____

_____

August 19

"When we cultivate a relationship with our essential nature,
we have an unshakable foundation upon which to build our life."
— TJ Woodward

MORNING

My intention for today is:

_____

_____

_____

NIGHTTIME

The high point of my day was:

_____

_____

_____

The low point of my day was:

_____

_____

_____

Today, I am (was) grateful for:

_____

_____

_____

August 20

*"Nothing can dim the light that
shines from within."*

— Maya Angelou

MORNING

My intention for today is:

_____

_____

_____

NIGHTTIME

The high point of my day was:

_____

_____

_____

The low point of my day was:

_____

_____

_____

Today, I am (was) grateful for:

_____

_____

_____

August 21

"We may be seeking love, but if we believe we are unlovable, we will create a frequency that attracts the absence of love."

— TJ Woodward

MORNING

My intention for today is:

_____

_____

_____

NIGHTTIME

The high point of my day was:

_____

_____

_____

The low point of my day was:

_____

_____

_____

Today, I am (was) grateful for:

_____

_____

_____

August 22

*"The only power our problems have over
us is the power we give to them."*

– Bob Proctor

MORNING

My intention for today is:

_____

_____

_____

NIGHTTIME

The high point of my day was:

_____

_____

_____

The low point of my day was:

_____

_____

_____

Today, I am (was) grateful for:

_____

_____

_____

August 23

*"Embracing the life of your dreams naturally emerges
as you radiate the energy of your vision."*

— TJ Woodward

MORNING

My intention for today is:

_____
_____
_____

NIGHTTIME

The high point of my day was:

_____
_____
_____

The low point of my day was:

_____
_____
_____

Today, I am (was) grateful for:

_____
_____
_____

August 24

"The true mark of maturity is when somebody hurts you and you try to understand their situation instead of hurting them back."

– Unknown

MORNING

My intention for today is:

_____

_____

_____

NIGHTTIME

The high point of my day was:

_____

_____

_____

The low point of my day was:

_____

_____

_____

Today, I am (was) grateful for:

_____

_____

_____

August 25

"Focus your inner ear not on the expected sound, but in the powerful messages you receive in the silence."
— TJ Woodward

MORNING

My intention for today is:

_____

_____

_____

NIGHTTIME

The high point of my day was:

_____

_____

_____

The low point of my day was:

_____

_____

_____

Today, I am (was) grateful for:

_____

_____

_____

August 26

"Experiencing peace means that you are capable of tapping into a blissful state of mind amidst the chaos of normal life."
– Jill Bolte Taylor

MORNING

My intention for today is:

_____

_____

_____

NIGHTTIME

The high point of my day was:

_____

_____

_____

The low point of my day was:

_____

_____

_____

Today, I am (was) grateful for:

_____

_____

_____

August 27

"The only past that actually exists is the past that exists in our mind. Knowing this is true freedom."

— TJ Woodward

MORNING

My intention for today is:

_____

_____

_____

NIGHTTIME

The high point of my day was:

_____

_____

_____

The low point of my day was:

_____

_____

_____

Today, I am (was) grateful for:

_____

_____

_____

August 28

"It is not joy that makes us grateful;
It's gratitude that makes us joyful."

– David Steindl-Rast

MORNING

My intention for today is:

_____

_____

_____

NIGHTTIME

The high point of my day was:

_____

_____

_____

The low point of my day was:

_____

_____

_____

Today, I am (was) grateful for:

_____

_____

_____

August 29

*"Is your past the book that you can't seem to put down,
the binge-worthy series that seems to never end?"*

— TJ Woodward

MORNING

My intention for today is:

_____

_____

_____

NIGHTTIME

The high point of my day was:

_____

_____

_____

The low point of my day was:

_____

_____

_____

Today, I am (was) grateful for:

_____

_____

_____

August 30

"There is no way to happiness.
Happiness is the way."

– Wayne Dyer

MORNING

My intention for today is:

_____

_____

_____

NIGHTTIME

The high point of my day was:

_____

_____

_____

The low point of my day was:

_____

_____

_____

Today, I am (was) grateful for:

_____

_____

_____

August 31

"Your perceived shortcomings are not the ultimate truth of who and what you are."

— TJ Woodward

MORNING

My intention for today is:

_____

_____

_____

NIGHTTIME

The high point of my day was:

_____

_____

_____

The low point of my day was:

_____

_____

_____

Today, I am (was) grateful for:

_____

_____

_____

September 1

"When we practice mindfulness we experience less limitation and more openness and curiosity."

– TJ Woodward

MORNING

My intention for today is:

_____

_____

_____

NIGHTTIME

The high point of my day was:

_____

_____

_____

The low point of my day was:

_____

_____

_____

Today, I am (was) grateful for:

_____

_____

_____

September 2

"You are free to choose, but you are not free from the consequences of your choice."

– Zig Ziglar

MORNING

My intention for today is:

_____

_____

_____

NIGHTTIME

The high point of my day was:

_____

_____

_____

The low point of my day was:

_____

_____

_____

Today, I am (was) grateful for:

_____

_____

_____

September 3

"There is no such thing as a negative emotion. They are sensations allowing us to recognize something needs attention."
– TJ Woodward

MORNING

My intention for today is:

_____

_____

_____

NIGHTTIME

The high point of my day was:

_____

_____

_____

The low point of my day was:

_____

_____

_____

Today, I am (was) grateful for:

_____

_____

_____

September 4

"Find the heart of it. Make the complex simple,
and you can achieve mastery."

– Dan Millman

MORNING

My intention for today is:

_____

_____

_____

NIGHTTIME

The high point of my day was:

_____

_____

_____

The low point of my day was:

_____

_____

_____

Today, I am (was) grateful for:

_____

_____

_____

September 5

"Living beyond our core false beliefs allows us to open up to the infinite potential of this moment."

— TJ Woodward

MORNING

My intention for today is:

_____

_____

_____

NIGHTTIME

The high point of my day was:

_____

_____

_____

The low point of my day was:

_____

_____

_____

Today, I am (was) grateful for:

_____

_____

_____

September 6

*"A single collective directed thought is all
it takes to change the world."*

– Lynne McTaggart

MORNING

My intention for today is:

_____

_____

_____

NIGHTTIME

The high point of my day was:

_____

_____

_____

The low point of my day was:

_____

_____

_____

Today, I am (was) grateful for:

_____

_____

_____

September 7

"Magic happens when we take full responsibility
for both our inner and outer lives."

– TJ Woodward

MORNING

My intention for today is:

_____

_____

_____

NIGHTTIME

The high point of my day was:

_____

_____

_____

The low point of my day was:

_____

_____

_____

Today, I am (was) grateful for:

_____

_____

_____

September 8

"It's not about action…
It's about vibrational alignment."

— Abraham Hicks

MORNING

My intention for today is:

_____

_____

_____

NIGHTTIME

The high point of my day was:

_____

_____

_____

The low point of my day was:

_____

_____

_____

Today, I am (was) grateful for:

_____

_____

_____

September 9

"Learning how to manage your racing thoughts allows you to stop perpetuating unnecessary drama."

– TJ Woodward

MORNING

My intention for today is:

_____

_____

_____

NIGHTTIME

The high point of my day was:

_____

_____

_____

The low point of my day was:

_____

_____

_____

Today, I am (was) grateful for:

_____

_____

_____

September 10

*"I began learning long ago that those who are happiest
are those who do the most for others."*

— Booker T. Washington

MORNING

My intention for today is:

_____

_____

_____

NIGHTTIME

The high point of my day was:

_____

_____

_____

The low point of my day was:

_____

_____

_____

Today, I am (was) grateful for:

_____

_____

_____

September 11

"You have the power within you to break free from life-long ideas that have kept you feeling stuck."

– TJ Woodward

MORNING

My intention for today is:

_____

_____

_____

NIGHTTIME

The high point of my day was:

_____

_____

_____

The low point of my day was:

_____

_____

_____

Today, I am (was) grateful for:

_____

_____

_____

September 12

"What if everything you're going through right now is preparing you for a dream bigger than you can imagine?"

– Unknown

MORNING

My intention for today is:

_____

_____

_____

NIGHTTIME

The high point of my day was:

_____

_____

_____

The low point of my day was:

_____

_____

_____

Today, I am (was) grateful for:

_____

_____

_____

September 13

"What are your unique skills, gifts, and talents that will help you fulfill the most magnificent vision for your life?"

— TJ Woodward

MORNING

My intention for today is:

_____

_____

_____

NIGHTTIME

The high point of my day was:

_____

_____

_____

The low point of my day was:

_____

_____

_____

Today, I am (was) grateful for:

_____

_____

_____

September 14

"Seriousness is equated with responsibility, when in fact, we would be much more responsible with more joy and laughter."
– Deepak Chopra

MORNING

My intention for today is:

_____

_____

_____

NIGHTTIME

The high point of my day was:

_____

_____

_____

The low point of my day was:

_____

_____

_____

Today, I am (was) grateful for:

_____

_____

_____

September 15

"Living in a state of grace is moving beyond cause and effect, and beyond the concepts of right and wrong."

— TJ Woodward

MORNING

My intention for today is:

_____

_____

_____

NIGHTTIME

The high point of my day was:

_____

_____

_____

The low point of my day was:

_____

_____

_____

Today, I am (was) grateful for:

_____

_____

_____

September 16

"Love: You're not meant to wait for it. You're not meant to search for it. You're meant to generate it."

– Michael Beckwith

MORNING

My intention for today is:

_____

_____

_____

NIGHTTIME

The high point of my day was:

_____

_____

_____

The low point of my day was:

_____

_____

_____

Today, I am (was) grateful for:

_____

_____

_____

September 17

"Want true freedom? Question every point of view you have about yourself and the world."

– TJ Woodward

MORNING

My intention for today is:

_____

_____

_____

NIGHTTIME

The high point of my day was:

_____

_____

_____

The low point of my day was:

_____

_____

_____

Today, I am (was) grateful for:

_____

_____

_____

September 18

"Get hooked on asking: Which thought feels better? Let the feeling of relief become most important to you."

— Unknown

MORNING

My intention for today is:

_____

_____

_____

NIGHTTIME

The high point of my day was:

_____

_____

_____

The low point of my day was:

_____

_____

_____

Today, I am (was) grateful for:

_____

_____

_____

September 19

*"As we radiate love frequency into the world,
life naturally responds."*

— TJ Woodward

MORNING

My intention for today is:

_____

_____

_____

NIGHTTIME

The high point of my day was:

_____

_____

_____

The low point of my day was:

_____

_____

_____

Today, I am (was) grateful for:

_____

_____

_____

September 20

"I have found that the most important thing in life is to stop saying 'I wish' and start saying 'I will'."

– David Copperfield

MORNING

My intention for today is:

_____

_____

_____

NIGHTTIME

The high point of my day was:

_____

_____

_____

The low point of my day was:

_____

_____

_____

Today, I am (was) grateful for:

_____

_____

_____

September 21

"The more you are aware of your oneness divine love, the easier it will be for you to let go of expectations and attachments."
— TJ Woodward

MORNING

My intention for today is:

_____

_____

_____

NIGHTTIME

The high point of my day was:

_____

_____

_____

The low point of my day was:

_____

_____

_____

Today, I am (was) grateful for:

_____

_____

_____

September 22

"The more difficult it is to forgive someone, the greater the opportunity for spiritual growth."
— Gabrielle Bernstein

MORNING

My intention for today is:

_____

_____

_____

NIGHTTIME

The high point of my day was:

_____

_____

_____

The low point of my day was:

_____

_____

_____

Today, I am (was) grateful for:

_____

_____

_____

September 23

*"When you have bravery to develop curiosity about what lies
in the shadow, you can access more love and compassion."*
— TJ Woodward

MORNING

My intention for today is:

_____

_____

_____

NIGHTTIME

The high point of my day was:

_____

_____

_____

The low point of my day was:

_____

_____

_____

Today, I am (was) grateful for:

_____

_____

_____

September 24

*"Every day gets better because what you want takes
on a stronger vibrational focus."*

— Unknown

MORNING

My intention for today is:

_____

_____

_____

NIGHTTIME

The high point of my day was:

_____

_____

_____

The low point of my day was:

_____

_____

_____

Today, I am (was) grateful for:

_____

_____

_____

September 25

"When we operate only in the visible realm, we're likely to feel like victims to the vicissitudes of life."

— TJ Woodward

MORNING

My intention for today is:

_____

_____

_____

NIGHTTIME

The high point of my day was:

_____

_____

_____

The low point of my day was:

_____

_____

_____

Today, I am (was) grateful for:

_____

_____

_____

September 26

*"The biggest adventure you can ever take
is to live the life of your dreams."*

— Oprah Winfrey

MORNING

My intention for today is:

_____

_____

_____

NIGHTTIME

The high point of my day was:

_____

_____

_____

The low point of my day was:

_____

_____

_____

Today, I am (was) grateful for:

_____

_____

_____

September 27

"With self-parenting, we discover how to talk in supportive ways to the parts of ourselves that feel wounded."

— TJ Woodward

MORNING

My intention for today is:

_____

_____

_____

NIGHTTIME

The high point of my day was:

_____

_____

_____

The low point of my day was:

_____

_____

_____

Today, I am (was) grateful for:

_____

_____

_____

September 28

*"Grace means that all of your mistakes now serve
a purpose instead of serving shame."*

— Brene Brown

MORNING

My intention for today is:

_____

_____

_____

NIGHTTIME

The high point of my day was:

_____

_____

_____

The low point of my day was:

_____

_____

_____

Today, I am (was) grateful for:

_____

_____

_____

September 29

"Through the practice of meditation, you can choose how to relate to your pain."

– TJ Woodward

MORNING

My intention for today is:

_____

_____

_____

NIGHTTIME

The high point of my day was:

_____

_____

_____

The low point of my day was:

_____

_____

_____

Today, I am (was) grateful for:

_____

_____

_____

September 30

"Despite how open and loving you attempt to be, people can only meet you as deeply as they've met themselves."

— Matt Kahn

MORNING

My intention for today is:

_____

_____

_____

NIGHTTIME

The high point of my day was:

_____

_____

_____

The low point of my day was:

_____

_____

_____

Today, I am (was) grateful for:

_____

_____

_____

October 1

"If you react to your thoughts without questioning them, you are only adding to the aggression of the world."

— TJ Woodward

MORNING

My intention for today is:

_____

_____

_____

NIGHTTIME

The high point of my day was:

_____

_____

_____

The low point of my day was:

_____

_____

_____

Today, I am (was) grateful for:

_____

_____

_____

October 2

"Our anxiety does not come from thinking about the future,
but from trying to control it."

– Kahlil Gibran

MORNING

My intention for today is:

_____

_____

_____

NIGHTTIME

The high point of my day was:

_____

_____

_____

The low point of my day was:

_____

_____

_____

Today, I am (was) grateful for:

_____

_____

_____

October 3

"Ultimately, the truth does not need to be found,
because it is already present within you."

— TJ Woodward

MORNING

My intention for today is:

_____

_____

_____

NIGHTTIME

The high point of my day was:

_____

_____

_____

The low point of my day was:

_____

_____

_____

Today, I am (was) grateful for:

_____

_____

_____

October 4

"The supreme act of forgiveness is when you can forgive yourself for all the wounds you've created in your life."

– Don Miguel Ruiz

MORNING

My intention for today is:

_____

_____

_____

NIGHTTIME

The high point of my day was:

_____

_____

_____

The low point of my day was:

_____

_____

_____

Today, I am (was) grateful for:

_____

_____

_____

October 5

"Cultivating a relationship with our true nature is the shortcut to ending our suffering."

— TJ Woodward

MORNING

My intention for today is:

_____

_____

_____

NIGHTTIME

The high point of my day was:

_____

_____

_____

The low point of my day was:

_____

_____

_____

Today, I am (was) grateful for:

_____

_____

_____

October 6

"Rather than always asking: 'What should I do?,'
we can reflect on: 'How should I be?'."

– Llewellyn Vaughan-Lee

MORNING

My intention for today is:

_____

_____

_____

NIGHTTIME

The high point of my day was:

_____

_____

_____

The low point of my day was:

_____

_____

_____

Today, I am (was) grateful for:

_____

_____

_____

October 7

"We don't actually become enlightened.
Enlightenment is revealed."

– TJ Woodward

MORNING

My intention for today is:

_____

_____

_____

NIGHTTIME

The high point of my day was:

_____

_____

_____

The low point of my day was:

_____

_____

_____

Today, I am (was) grateful for:

_____

_____

_____

October 8

"You're not here to have a relationship with others. You're here to have a relationship with source."

— Unknown

MORNING

My intention for today is:

_____

_____

_____

NIGHTTIME

The high point of my day was:

_____

_____

_____

The low point of my day was:

_____

_____

_____

Today, I am (was) grateful for:

_____

_____

_____

October 9

*"Fear and worry are effectively your unresolved
past imagined in the future."*

– TJ Woodward

MORNING

My intention for today is:

_____

_____

_____

NIGHTTIME

The high point of my day was:

_____

_____

_____

The low point of my day was:

_____

_____

_____

Today, I am (was) grateful for:

_____

_____

_____

October 10

"The truth cannot be captured by concept;
reality begins where all words end."

– Zen Thinking

MORNING

My intention for today is:

_____

_____

_____

NIGHTTIME

The high point of my day was:

_____

_____

_____

The low point of my day was:

_____

_____

_____

Today, I am (was) grateful for:

_____

_____

_____

October 11

"What you imagine others are thinking about you
is a window into your own self-image."

– TJ Woodward

MORNING

My intention for today is:

_____

_____

_____

NIGHTTIME

The high point of my day was:

_____

_____

_____

The low point of my day was:

_____

_____

_____

Today, I am (was) grateful for:

_____

_____

_____

October 12

"The entire universe compensates and adjusts to your vibration. You're that special."

– Unknown

MORNING

My intention for today is:

_____

_____

_____

NIGHTTIME

The high point of my day was:

_____

_____

_____

The low point of my day was:

_____

_____

_____

Today, I am (was) grateful for:

_____

_____

_____

October 13

*"Even a momentary glimpse into ultimate reality
creates a softening of the ego."*

– TJ Woodward

MORNING

My intention for today is:

_____

_____

_____

NIGHTTIME

The high point of my day was:

_____

_____

_____

The low point of my day was:

_____

_____

_____

Today, I am (was) grateful for:

_____

_____

_____

October 14

*"Hold fast to your vision and do something every day
to bring it into manifestation."*

– Michael Beckwith

MORNING

My intention for today is:

_____

_____

_____

NIGHTTIME

The high point of my day was:

_____

_____

_____

The low point of my day was:

_____

_____

_____

Today, I am (was) grateful for:

_____

_____

_____

October 15

"When you understand the truth of your being, the details of your life become less significant."

— TJ Woodward

MORNING

My intention for today is:

_____

_____

_____

NIGHTTIME

The high point of my day was:

_____

_____

_____

The low point of my day was:

_____

_____

_____

Today, I am (was) grateful for:

_____

_____

_____

October 16

"There can only be one solution to any problem:
a change in attitude and consciousness."

– Gregg Braden

MORNING

My intention for today is:

_____

_____

_____

NIGHTTIME

The high point of my day was:

_____

_____

_____

The low point of my day was:

_____

_____

_____

Today, I am (was) grateful for:

_____

_____

_____

October 17

"The authentic spiritual journey is not a destination,
it is an inner discovery."

– TJ Woodward

MORNING

My intention for today is:

_____

_____

_____

NIGHTTIME

The high point of my day was:

_____

_____

_____

The low point of my day was:

_____

_____

_____

Today, I am (was) grateful for:

_____

_____

_____

October 18

"And I said to my body, softly: 'I want to be your friend.' It took a long breath and replied: 'I've been waiting all my life for this.'"
— Nayyrah Waheed

MORNING

My intention for today is:

_____

_____

_____

NIGHTTIME

The high point of my day was:

_____

_____

_____

The low point of my day was:

_____

_____

_____

Today, I am (was) grateful for:

_____

_____

_____

October 19

"Take a deep breath. Question every point of view.
Reflect on your true nature."

– TJ Woodward

MORNING

My intention for today is:

_____

_____

_____

NIGHTTIME

The high point of my day was:

_____

_____

_____

The low point of my day was:

_____

_____

_____

Today, I am (was) grateful for:

_____

_____

_____

October 20

"What are you willing to give up, in order to become who you need to be?"

– Elizabeth Gilbert

MORNING

My intention for today is:

_____

_____

_____

NIGHTTIME

The high point of my day was:

_____

_____

_____

The low point of my day was:

_____

_____

_____

Today, I am (was) grateful for:

_____

_____

_____

October 21

"We have become so identified with the central story of our past that we don't know who we are in the present."

– TJ Woodward

MORNING

My intention for today is:

_____

_____

_____

NIGHTTIME

The high point of my day was:

_____

_____

_____

The low point of my day was:

_____

_____

_____

Today, I am (was) grateful for:

_____

_____

_____

October 22

"Every emotion naturally arises and subsides. Your role is to simply witness what is happening without judgment."
— Panache Desai

MORNING

My intention for today is:

_____

_____

_____

NIGHTTIME

The high point of my day was:

_____

_____

_____

The low point of my day was:

_____

_____

_____

Today, I am (was) grateful for:

_____

_____

_____

October 23

"We don't need to earn love, because love is the ultimate truth of who and what we are."

— TJ Woodward

MORNING

My intention for today is:

_____

_____

_____

NIGHTTIME

The high point of my day was:

_____

_____

_____

The low point of my day was:

_____

_____

_____

Today, I am (was) grateful for:

_____

_____

_____

October 24

"Step into the fire of self-discovery. This fire will not burn you, it will only burn what you are not."

— Mooji

MORNING

My intention for today is:

_____

_____

_____

NIGHTTIME

The high point of my day was:

_____

_____

_____

The low point of my day was:

_____

_____

_____

Today, I am (was) grateful for:

_____

_____

_____

October 25

"An awareness of our true nature can happen in an instant, then we might spend our whole life trying to understand it."

— TJ Woodward

MORNING

My intention for today is:

_____

_____

_____

NIGHTTIME

The high point of my day was:

_____

_____

_____

The low point of my day was:

_____

_____

_____

Today, I am (was) grateful for:

_____

_____

_____

October 26

"Once you learn how to create your own happiness,
no one can take it from you."

— Robert Tew

MORNING

My intention for today is:

_____

_____

_____

NIGHTTIME

The high point of my day was:

_____

_____

_____

The low point of my day was:

_____

_____

_____

Today, I am (was) grateful for:

_____

_____

_____

October 27

*"Any perceived enemy is simply showing us the
possibility of deeper healing."*

– TJ Woodward

MORNING

My intention for today is:

_____

_____

_____

NIGHTTIME

The high point of my day was:

_____

_____

_____

The low point of my day was:

_____

_____

_____

Today, I am (was) grateful for:

_____

_____

_____

October 28

*"Do something today that your future
self will thank you for."*

– Unknown

MORNING

My intention for today is:

_____

_____

_____

NIGHTTIME

The high point of my day was:

_____

_____

_____

The low point of my day was:

_____

_____

_____

Today, I am (was) grateful for:

_____

_____

_____

October 29

"Giving into the magnetic pull of the past is living in a state of the imagined not now."

– TJ Woodward

MORNING

My intention for today is:

_____

_____

_____

NIGHTTIME

The high point of my day was:

_____

_____

_____

The low point of my day was:

_____

_____

_____

Today, I am (was) grateful for:

_____

_____

_____

October 30

*"You can choose courage or you can choose comfort.
You cannot have both."*

– Brene Brown

MORNING

My intention for today is:

_____

_____

_____

NIGHTTIME

The high point of my day was:

_____

_____

_____

The low point of my day was:

_____

_____

_____

Today, I am (was) grateful for:

_____

_____

_____

October 31

"How can we be at peace with others?
There are no others."

– TJ Woodward

MORNING

My intention for today is:

_____

_____

_____

NIGHTTIME

The high point of my day was:

_____

_____

_____

The low point of my day was:

_____

_____

_____

Today, I am (was) grateful for:

_____

_____

_____

November 1

*"Quite often, we see and judge in others what
we refuse to accept about ourselves."*

– TJ Woodward

MORNING

My intention for today is:

_____

_____

_____

NIGHTTIME

The high point of my day was:

_____

_____

_____

The low point of my day was:

_____

_____

_____

Today, I am (was) grateful for:

_____

_____

_____

November 2

"I sat inside a room with nothing in it and realized it was still full. This is when I knew I was enough."

– Rudy Francisco

MORNING

My intention for today is:

_____

_____

_____

NIGHTTIME

The high point of my day was:

_____

_____

_____

The low point of my day was:

_____

_____

_____

Today, I am (was) grateful for:

_____

_____

_____

November 3

"Feelings are more neutral than you might have imagined.
It's your attachment to them that creates suffering."

— TJ Woodward

MORNING

My intention for today is:

_____

_____

_____

NIGHTTIME

The high point of my day was:

_____

_____

_____

The low point of my day was:

_____

_____

_____

Today, I am (was) grateful for:

_____

_____

_____

November 4

"The thing I remember most about the successful people I've met is their obvious delight in what they're doing."

– Fred Rogers

MORNING

My intention for today is:

_____

_____

_____

NIGHTTIME

The high point of my day was:

_____

_____

_____

The low point of my day was:

_____

_____

_____

Today, I am (was) grateful for:

_____

_____

_____

November 5

"Spiritual evolution is not moving toward some perfect state, it is growing in awareness of a perfection that already is."
— TJ Woodward

MORNING

My intention for today is:

_____

_____

_____

NIGHTTIME

The high point of my day was:

_____

_____

_____

The low point of my day was:

_____

_____

_____

Today, I am (was) grateful for:

_____

_____

_____

November 6

"All doubt and fear become insignificant once the intention of life becomes love."

— Rumi

MORNING

My intention for today is:

_____

_____

_____

NIGHTTIME

The high point of my day was:

_____

_____

_____

The low point of my day was:

_____

_____

_____

Today, I am (was) grateful for:

_____

_____

_____

November 7

"We don't need to take on the identity of a victim,
regardless of what has happened in our past."

— TJ Woodward

MORNING

My intention for today is:

_____

_____

_____

NIGHTTIME

The high point of my day was:

_____

_____

_____

The low point of my day was:

_____

_____

_____

Today, I am (was) grateful for:

_____

_____

_____

November 8

"Beware of the destination addiction. Until you give up the idea that happiness is somewhere else, it will never happen."

– Robert Holden

MORNING

My intention for today is:

_____

_____

_____

NIGHTTIME

The high point of my day was:

_____

_____

_____

The low point of my day was:

_____

_____

_____

Today, I am (was) grateful for:

_____

_____

_____

November 9

"Cease defining yourself and you will naturally experience oneness with all of life."

— TJ Woodward

MORNING

My intention for today is:

_____

_____

_____

NIGHTTIME

The high point of my day was:

_____

_____

_____

The low point of my day was:

_____

_____

_____

Today, I am (was) grateful for:

_____

_____

_____

November 10

"Forgive yourself for not being at peace. The moment you completely accept your non-peace it is transformed into peace."
– Unknown

MORNING

My intention for today is:

_____

_____

_____

NIGHTTIME

The high point of my day was:

_____

_____

_____

The low point of my day was:

_____

_____

_____

Today, I am (was) grateful for:

_____

_____

_____

November 11

"Have you been searching for a miracle?
Perhaps it's time to look in the mirror."

— TJ Woodward

MORNING

My intention for today is:

_____

_____

_____

NIGHTTIME

The high point of my day was:

_____

_____

_____

The low point of my day was:

_____

_____

_____

Today, I am (was) grateful for:

_____

_____

_____

November 12

*"The most important aspect of love is not in the giving
or receiving; it is in the being."*

— Ram Dass

MORNING

My intention for today is:

_____

_____

_____

NIGHTTIME

The high point of my day was:

_____

_____

_____

The low point of my day was:

_____

_____

_____

Today, I am (was) grateful for:

_____

_____

_____

November 13

"At the deepest level, we all want to experience love and connection."

— TJ Woodward

MORNING

My intention for today is:

_____

_____

_____

NIGHTTIME

The high point of my day was:

_____

_____

_____

The low point of my day was:

_____

_____

_____

Today, I am (was) grateful for:

_____

_____

_____

November 14

"The substance of everything is the divine. This is not something you believe, it's something you realize."

– Adyashanti

MORNING

My intention for today is:

_____

_____

_____

NIGHTTIME

The high point of my day was:

_____

_____

_____

The low point of my day was:

_____

_____

_____

Today, I am (was) grateful for:

_____

_____

_____

November 15

"Awakening in its simplest form is waking up from the illusion of separateness."

— TJ Woodward

MORNING

My intention for today is:

_____

_____

_____

NIGHTTIME

The high point of my day was:

_____

_____

_____

The low point of my day was:

_____

_____

_____

Today, I am (was) grateful for:

_____

_____

_____

November 16

*"When we know what to do with the contractions we feel,
we start to dance with the experiences of life."*

– Dr. Sue Morter

MORNING

My intention for today is:

_____

_____

_____

NIGHTTIME

The high point of my day was:

_____

_____

_____

The low point of my day was:

_____

_____

_____

Today, I am (was) grateful for:

_____

_____

_____

November 17

*"Joy is your natural state. Release what is
untrue and reside in it."*

— TJ Woodward

MORNING

My intention for today is:

_____

_____

_____

NIGHTTIME

The high point of my day was:

_____

_____

_____

The low point of my day was:

_____

_____

_____

Today, I am (was) grateful for:

_____

_____

_____

November 18

"Surround yourself with people who talk about visions and ideas, not other people."

– Unknown

MORNING

My intention for today is:

_____

_____

_____

NIGHTTIME

The high point of my day was:

_____

_____

_____

The low point of my day was:

_____

_____

_____

Today, I am (was) grateful for:

_____

_____

_____

November 19

*"Life's perceived challenges are an invitation
to your greatest awakening."*

– TJ Woodward

MORNING

My intention for today is:

_____

_____

_____

NIGHTTIME

The high point of my day was:

_____

_____

_____

The low point of my day was:

_____

_____

_____

Today, I am (was) grateful for:

_____

_____

_____

November 20

"We won't be distracted by comparison if
we are captivated with purpose."

– Unknown

MORNING

My intention for today is:

_____

_____

_____

NIGHTTIME

The high point of my day was:

_____

_____

_____

The low point of my day was:

_____

_____

_____

Today, I am (was) grateful for:

_____

_____

_____

November 21

"When we are able to relax into not knowing,
we experience true safety."

– TJ Woodward

MORNING

My intention for today is:

_____

_____

_____

NIGHTTIME

The high point of my day was:

_____

_____

_____

The low point of my day was:

_____

_____

_____

Today, I am (was) grateful for:

_____

_____

_____

November 22

*"What appears to be an emergency is really
the next stage of your evolution."*

– Michael Beckwith

MORNING

My intention for today is:

_____

_____

_____

NIGHTTIME

The high point of my day was:

_____

_____

_____

The low point of my day was:

_____

_____

_____

Today, I am (was) grateful for:

_____

_____

_____

November 23

"The greatest gift we can offer the world right now is to commit to our own transformation."

– TJ Woodward

MORNING

My intention for today is:

_____

_____

_____

NIGHTTIME

The high point of my day was:

_____

_____

_____

The low point of my day was:

_____

_____

_____

Today, I am (was) grateful for:

_____

_____

_____

November 24

"There are opportunities everywhere,
just as there have always been."

– Charles Fillmore

MORNING

My intention for today is:

_____

_____

_____

NIGHTTIME

The high point of my day was:

_____

_____

_____

The low point of my day was:

_____

_____

_____

Today, I am (was) grateful for:

_____

_____

_____

November 25

*"Scientists are proving what mystics have known for centuries –
that everything is an expression of one life."*

— TJ Woodward

MORNING

My intention for today is:

_____

_____

_____

NIGHTTIME

The high point of my day was:

_____

_____

_____

The low point of my day was:

_____

_____

_____

Today, I am (was) grateful for:

_____

_____

_____

November 26

"Many personal problems you perceive are merely dreams of the mind, caused by a relationship problem with yourself."

– Zen Thinking

MORNING

My intention for today is:

_____

_____

_____

NIGHTTIME

The high point of my day was:

_____

_____

_____

The low point of my day was:

_____

_____

_____

Today, I am (was) grateful for:

_____

_____

_____

November 27

"It requires courage to relinquish truths that were once useful but now hold us back."

– TJ Woodward

MORNING

My intention for today is:

_____

_____

_____

NIGHTTIME

The high point of my day was:

_____

_____

_____

The low point of my day was:

_____

_____

_____

Today, I am (was) grateful for:

_____

_____

_____

November 28

*"Learn to honor the space between
no longer and not yet."*

— Nancy Levin

MORNING

My intention for today is:

_____

_____

_____

NIGHTTIME

The high point of my day was:

_____

_____

_____

The low point of my day was:

_____

_____

_____

Today, I am (was) grateful for:

_____

_____

_____

November 29

*"The spiritual path isn't about changing yourself,
it is about loving yourself."*

— TJ Woodward

MORNING

My intention for today is:

_____

_____

_____

NIGHTTIME

The high point of my day was:

_____

_____

_____

The low point of my day was:

_____

_____

_____

Today, I am (was) grateful for:

_____

_____

_____

November 30

*"You are the only person on earth who
can use your specific abilities."*

– Zig Ziglar

MORNING

My intention for today is:

_____

_____

_____

NIGHTTIME

The high point of my day was:

_____

_____

_____

The low point of my day was:

_____

_____

_____

Today, I am (was) grateful for:

_____

_____

_____

December 1

*"Suffering ceases when we are willing to fully accept
the whole gamut of our emotions."*

– TJ Woodward

MORNING

My intention for today is:

_____

_____

_____

NIGHTTIME

The high point of my day was:

_____

_____

_____

The low point of my day was:

_____

_____

_____

Today, I am (was) grateful for:

_____

_____

_____

December 2

"Use me, God. Show me how to take who I am and what I can do, and use it for a purpose greater than myself."

– Martin Luther King Jr.

MORNING

My intention for today is:

_____

_____

_____

NIGHTTIME

The high point of my day was:

_____

_____

_____

The low point of my day was:

_____

_____

_____

Today, I am (was) grateful for:

_____

_____

_____

December 3

"We are not the sum total of our experiences,
but the meaning we give to them."

— TJ Woodward

MORNING

My intention for today is:

_____

_____

_____

NIGHTTIME

The high point of my day was:

_____

_____

_____

The low point of my day was:

_____

_____

_____

Today, I am (was) grateful for:

_____

_____

_____

December 4

"To forgive is to set a prisoner free and discover that the prisoner was you."

– Lewis B. Smedes

MORNING

My intention for today is:

_____

_____

_____

NIGHTTIME

The high point of my day was:

_____

_____

_____

The low point of my day was:

_____

_____

_____

Today, I am (was) grateful for:

_____

_____

_____

December 5

"Peace is not a destination.
It is a way of being."

— TJ Woodward

MORNING

My intention for today is:

_____

_____

_____

NIGHTTIME

The high point of my day was:

_____

_____

_____

The low point of my day was:

_____

_____

_____

Today, I am (was) grateful for:

_____

_____

_____

December 6

"Spread love wherever you go. Let no one ever come to you without leaving happier."

— Mother Teresa

MORNING

My intention for today is:

_____

_____

_____

NIGHTTIME

The high point of my day was:

_____

_____

_____

The low point of my day was:

_____

_____

_____

Today, I am (was) grateful for:

_____

_____

_____

December 7

"When we are spiritually awakened, the personality becomes a vehicle for spirit."

– TJ Woodward

MORNING

My intention for today is:

_____

_____

_____

NIGHTTIME

The high point of my day was:

_____

_____

_____

The low point of my day was:

_____

_____

_____

Today, I am (was) grateful for:

_____

_____

_____

December 8

"You stop explaining yourself when you realize people only understand from their level of perception."

– Jim Carrey

MORNING

My intention for today is:

_____

_____

_____

NIGHTTIME

The high point of my day was:

_____

_____

_____

The low point of my day was:

_____

_____

_____

Today, I am (was) grateful for:

_____

_____

_____

December 9

"If our doing is not rooted in being, it is like building a house on sand rather than solid ground."

– TJ Woodward

MORNING

My intention for today is:

_____

_____

_____

NIGHTTIME

The high point of my day was:

_____

_____

_____

The low point of my day was:

_____

_____

_____

Today, I am (was) grateful for:

_____

_____

_____

December 10

"It is very rare or almost impossible that an event can be seen as negative from all points of view ."

– The Dalai Lama

MORNING

My intention for today is:

_____

_____

_____

NIGHTTIME

The high point of my day was:

_____

_____

_____

The low point of my day was:

_____

_____

_____

Today, I am (was) grateful for:

_____

_____

_____

December 11

*"Living on purpose is achieved when we find
balance between being and doing."*

— TJ Woodward

MORNING

My intention for today is:

_____

_____

_____

NIGHTTIME

The high point of my day was:

_____

_____

_____

The low point of my day was:

_____

_____

_____

Today, I am (was) grateful for:

_____

_____

_____

December 12

*"Everything that happens to you is a reflection of
what you believe about yourself."*

– Iyanla Vanzant

MORNING

My intention for today is:

_____

_____

_____

NIGHTTIME

The high point of my day was:

_____

_____

_____

The low point of my day was:

_____

_____

_____

Today, I am (was) grateful for:

_____

_____

_____

December 13

"In meditation, we experience a freedom that we cannot possibly know when we are confined within the constructs of our mind."
— TJ Woodward

MORNING

My intention for today is:

_____

_____

_____

NIGHTTIME

The high point of my day was:

_____

_____

_____

The low point of my day was:

_____

_____

_____

Today, I am (was) grateful for:

_____

_____

_____

December 14

"The thoughts we choose to think are the tools we use
to paint the canvas of our lives."

— Louise Hay

MORNING

My intention for today is:

_____

_____

_____

NIGHTTIME

The high point of my day was:

_____

_____

_____

The low point of my day was:

_____

_____

_____

Today, I am (was) grateful for:

_____

_____

_____

December 15

"Living in a question opens us up to infinite possibilities rather than keeping us stuck in our normal way of seeing things."
— TJ Woodward

MORNING

My intention for today is:

_____

_____

_____

NIGHTTIME

The high point of my day was:

_____

_____

_____

The low point of my day was:

_____

_____

_____

Today, I am (was) grateful for:

_____

_____

_____

December 16

"A comfort zone is a beautiful place, but nothing grows there. Life begins at the end of your comfort zone."

– Unknown

MORNING

My intention for today is:

_____

_____

_____

NIGHTTIME

The high point of my day was:

_____

_____

_____

The low point of my day was:

_____

_____

_____

Today, I am (was) grateful for:

_____

_____

_____

December 17

"When we expect a romantic partner to fill our emptiness, we create a relationship based on dependency and fear of loss."
— TJ Woodward

MORNING

My intention for today is:

_____

_____

_____

NIGHTTIME

The high point of my day was:

_____

_____

_____

The low point of my day was:

_____

_____

_____

Today, I am (was) grateful for:

_____

_____

_____

December 18

"You are participating in your
own unfolding destiny."

– Michael Beckwith

MORNING

My intention for today is:

_____

_____

_____

NIGHTTIME

The high point of my day was:

_____

_____

_____

The low point of my day was:

_____

_____

_____

Today, I am (was) grateful for:

_____

_____

_____

December 19

"When the student is ready the teacher will appear. When the student is REALLY ready, the teacher will disappear."

– TJ Woodward

MORNING

My intention for today is:

_____

_____

_____

NIGHTTIME

The high point of my day was:

_____

_____

_____

The low point of my day was:

_____

_____

_____

Today, I am (was) grateful for:

_____

_____

_____

December 20

"Replace 'I'm sorry' with 'thank you.' So, instead of saying 'sorry I was late' say 'thank you for waiting for me.'"

– Unknown

MORNING

My intention for today is:

_____

_____

_____

NIGHTTIME

The high point of my day was:

_____

_____

_____

The low point of my day was:

_____

_____

_____

Today, I am (was) grateful for:

_____

_____

_____

December 21

*"Stillness is found beyond all the
dualities the mind creates."*

– TJ Woodward

MORNING

My intention for today is:

_____

_____

_____

NIGHTTIME

The high point of my day was:

_____

_____

_____

The low point of my day was:

_____

_____

_____

Today, I am (was) grateful for:

_____

_____

_____

December 22

"People often say that gratitude doesn't last. Well, neither does bathing. That's why we recommend practicing it daily."

— Unknown

MORNING

My intention for today is:

_____

_____

_____

NIGHTTIME

The high point of my day was:

_____

_____

_____

The low point of my day was:

_____

_____

_____

Today, I am (was) grateful for:

_____

_____

_____

December 23

"Teachers, books, and philosophies can point us toward the truth, but in the end, it is only discovered within oneself."

— TJ Woodward

MORNING

My intention for today is:

_____

_____

_____

NIGHTTIME

The high point of my day was:

_____

_____

_____

The low point of my day was:

_____

_____

_____

Today, I am (was) grateful for:

_____

_____

_____

December 24

"If you want something you've never had,
You have to do something you've never done."

— Unknown

MORNING

My intention for today is:

_____

_____

_____

NIGHTTIME

The high point of my day was:

_____

_____

_____

The low point of my day was:

_____

_____

_____

Today, I am (was) grateful for:

_____

_____

_____

December 25

"We are in a unique time in history where lasting peace can prevail because enough of us are ready to create harmony."

— TJ Woodward

MORNING

My intention for today is:

_____

_____

_____

NIGHTTIME

The high point of my day was:

_____

_____

_____

The low point of my day was:

_____

_____

_____

Today, I am (was) grateful for:

_____

_____

_____

December 26

*"How exciting it is to be
surrounded by possibilities."*

– Sandra Ann Taylor

MORNING

My intention for today is:

_____

_____

_____

NIGHTTIME

The high point of my day was:

_____

_____

_____

The low point of my day was:

_____

_____

_____

Today, I am (was) grateful for:

_____

_____

_____

December 27

"By choosing to express compassion in the face of another's pain, we are changing the emotional climate of the world."
— TJ Woodward

MORNING

My intention for today is:

_____

_____

_____

NIGHTTIME

The high point of my day was:

_____

_____

_____

The low point of my day was:

_____

_____

_____

Today, I am (was) grateful for:

_____

_____

_____

December 28

"Spirituality is meant to take us beyond our tribal identity into a domain of awareness that is more universal."

– Deepak Chopra

MORNING

My intention for today is:

_____

_____

_____

NIGHTTIME

The high point of my day was:

_____

_____

_____

The low point of my day was:

_____

_____

_____

Today, I am (was) grateful for:

_____

_____

_____

December 29

*"A gentle reminder of the truth: You are peace. You are love.
You are light. You are the one you've been waiting for."*

— TJ Woodward

MORNING

My intention for today is:

_____

_____

_____

NIGHTTIME

The high point of my day was:

_____

_____

_____

The low point of my day was:

_____

_____

_____

Today, I am (was) grateful for:

_____

_____

_____

December 30

"The connections we make in the course of a life –
maybe that's what heaven is."

– Fred Rogers

MORNING

My intention for today is:

_____

_____

_____

NIGHTTIME

The high point of my day was:

_____

_____

_____

The low point of my day was:

_____

_____

_____

Today, I am (was) grateful for:

_____

_____

_____

December 31

"You are here to open your heart to a new way of being. The moment is now."

— TJ Woodward

MORNING

My intention for today is:

_____

_____

_____

NIGHTTIME

The high point of my day was:

_____

_____

_____

The low point of my day was:

_____

_____

_____

Today, I am (was) grateful for:

_____

_____

_____

ADDITIONAL JOURNALING/NOTES

ADDITIONAL JOURNALING/NOTES

ADDITIONAL JOURNALING/NOTES

ADDITIONAL JOURNALING/NOTES

ADDITIONAL JOURNALING/NOTES

ADDITIONAL JOURNALING/NOTES

ADDITIONAL JOURNALING/NOTES

ADDITIONAL JOURNALING/NOTES

ADDITIONAL JOURNALING/NOTES

ADDITIONAL JOURNALING/NOTES

ADDITIONAL JOURNALING/NOTES

ADDITIONAL JOURNALING/NOTES

ADDITIONAL JOURNALING/NOTES

ADDITIONAL JOURNALING/NOTES

ADDITIONAL JOURNALING/NOTES

CONGRATULATIONS!

Thank you so much for your wiliness to engage in this journal.

Sending you love and light!

TJ Woodward

www.ConsciousRecovery.com

Made in the USA
Las Vegas, NV
23 September 2023